Modern and Contemporary Poetry and Poetics

Series Editor
Ann Vickery
Deakin University
Burwood, Australia

Founded by Rachel Blau DuPlessis, continued by David Herd, and now headed by Ann Vickery, *Modern and Contemporary Poetry and Poetics* promotes and pursues topicsin the burgeoning field of 20th and 21st century poetics. Critical and scholarly work on poetry and poetics of interestto the series includes: social location in its relationships to subjectivity, to the construction of authorship, to oeuvres,and to careers; poetic reception and dissemination (groups, movements, formations, institutions); the intersection ofpoetry and theory; questions about language, poetic authority, and the goals of writing; claims in poetics, impacts ofsocial life, and the dynamics of the poetic career as these are staged and debated by poets and inside poems. Since its inception, the series has been distinguished by its tilt toward experimental work – intellectually, politically, aesthetically. It has consistently published work on Anglophone poetry in the broadest sense and has featured critical work studying literatures of the UK, of the US, of Canada, and Australia, as well as eclectic mixes of work from other social and poetic communities. As poetry and poetics form a crucial response to contemporary social and political conditions, under David Herd's editorship the series will continue to broaden understanding of the field and its significance.

Editorial Board Members:
Rachel Blau DuPlessis, Temple University
Vincent Broqua, Université Paris 8
Olivier Brossard, Université Paris-Est
Steve Collis, Simon Fraser University
Jacob Edmond, University of Otago
Stephen Fredman, Notre Dame University
Fiona Green, University of Cambridge
Abigail Lang, Université Paris Diderot
Will Montgomery, Royal Holloway University of London
Miriam Nichols, University of the Fraser Valley
Redell Olsen, Royal Holloway University of London
Sandeep Parmar, University of Liverpool
Adam Piette, University of Sheffield
Nisha Ramaya, Queen Mary University of London
Brian Reed, University of Washington
Carol Watts, University of Sussex

Travis W. Matteson

Emergent Poetics

Ecological Sites in Contemporary Poetry

Travis W. Matteson
SUNY Alfred State College
Alfred, NY, USA

ISSN 2634-6052 ISSN 2634-6060 (electronic)
Modern and Contemporary Poetry and Poetics
ISBN 978-3-031-70736-0 ISBN 978-3-031-70737-7 (eBook)
https://doi.org/10.1007/978-3-031-70737-7

© The Editor(s) (if applicable) and The Author(s), under exclusive license to Springer Nature Switzerland AG 2025

This work is subject to copyright. All rights are solely and exclusively licensed by the Publisher, whether the whole or part of the material is concerned, specifically the rights of translation, reprinting, reuse of illustrations, recitation, broadcasting, reproduction on microfilms or in any other physical way, and transmission or information storage and retrieval, electronic adaptation, computer software, or by similar or dissimilar methodology now known or hereafter developed.
The use of general descriptive names, registered names, trademarks, service marks, etc. in this publication does not imply, even in the absence of a specific statement, that such names are exempt from the relevant protective laws and regulations and therefore free for general use.
The publisher, the authors and the editors are safe to assume that the advice and information in this book are believed to be true and accurate at the date of publication. Neither the publisher nor the authors or the editors give a warranty, expressed or implied, with respect to the material contained herein or for any errors or omissions that may have been made. The publisher remains neutral with regard to jurisdictional claims in published maps and institutional affiliations.

This Palgrave Macmillan imprint is published by the registered company Springer Nature Switzerland AG.
The registered company address is: Gewerbestrasse 11, 6330 Cham, Switzerland

If disposing of this product, please recycle the paper.

I would like to dedicate this book to Sarabeth, Amelia, Henry, and Eliza for their patience and support

Contents

1. **Introduction** — 1
   References — 15

2. **Photogram as Poetic Method: Susan Howe's Materialist Telepathy** — 17
   2.1 *A Gentle Realism* — 18
   2.2 *A Shadow That Is a Shadow Of* — 25
   2.3 *Mystic Documentary Telepathy* — 35
   2.4 *The Ghost in the Archive* — 39
   2.5 *Rien négligé* — 45
   References — 47

3. **Deep Erasure in Yedda Morrison's Darkness** — 51
   3.1 *Activating the Scenery* — 52
   3.2 *Genre Trouble* — 59
   3.3 *Man / the Chosen* — 63
   3.4 *Metaphors on* Darkness — 69
   3.5 *Bewildering the Medium* — 74
   3.6 *Among the Being of Being* — 79
   References — 79

4   Environmental Textuality in the Ambient Web   83
    4.1   Ambience Is a [Medium]   84
    4.2   Some Sort of Plagiarized Accounting   89
    4.3   Against Resistance   95
    4.4   Exteriorizing the Ecosystem   102
    References   107

5   Conclusion: Starting from Nothing   111
    References   114

Index   115

CHAPTER 1

Introduction

No scholar has captured the spirit of the moment in such vivid and occasionally combative terms as Bruno Latour, who claimed in 2004 that critique had "run out of steam" (225). The thrust of Latour's argument is that institutional critique, at the same time as it has been appropriated by ideologues (his example is climate change deniers), has outlived both its usefulness at resisting institutional structures and its accuracy at representing agency and power relationships in the real world. In response to Latour's diagnosis, many theorists—particularly those in the literary media studies—have offered engaging and fruitful alternatives to (or reappraisals of) traditional critique, but in this project, I suggest that literary criticism should follow rather than lead. The most compelling and constructive alternatives to critique today are to be found in contemporary innovative poetics.

Gerald Bruns defines a particular vein of contemporary poetry he calls poetic materialism: "poetry that seems to insert itself into the everyday world of banal objects, where it abides as one thing among others" (2012, p. 4). This project is concerned with this loosely connected movement, in the ways these poetries self-reflexively comment on their own physical properties and mediated existence, and their relationship to their larger material networks. Crucially, according to Bruns, this materialist poetry is less metaphorical—specifically, less invested in the figurative aspects of language as an indirect representation of experience or emotion and more invested in the medium-specific, literal existence of the poem itself as an object among other objects (2012, pp. 88, 91). Bruns follows Charles Bernstein in emphasizing a shift from the intellectual materiality of language to the social materiality of language, from a focus on the rhetorical features of language (especially metaphor) to a focus on what could be called the poem's social network: histories and material cultures into which a poem enters and (often) from which it appropriates (2012, p. 31).

This poetic materialism is self-consciously a response to both conventional poetry and conventional literary criticism, both of which are often guilty of a linguistic anthropocentrism, in which things in the world exist as mere containers for human ideologies, and every problem is reduced to a problem of discourse. Subordinating the physical world to the linguistic world denies objects their materiality, their reality, and if objects are denied reality in language, they can be denied reality in practice. As Jane Bennett writes in *Vibrant Matter: A Political Ecology of Things*, "Dead or instrumentalized matter feeds human hubris and our earth-destroying fantasies of conquest and consumption" (2010, p. ix). Timothy Morton puts it this way: "This [capitalist] materialism treats the world as objective stuff to be manipulated by disembodied subjects" (2002, p. 55). De-materializing objects, or entire planets, justifies their exploitation and destruction for human purposes. Consider the term "media ecology," a systems metaphor meant to provide insight into how human communication platforms relate to each other. One example of an application of media-ecological metaphors in literary studies is Kenneth Goldsmith's concept of a "textual ecosystem": borrowing James Joyce's writing on the properties of water in *Ulysses*, Goldsmith draws an analogy between the water cycle and the different "phases" of digital language (2011, p. 27). By metaphorizing water, Goldsmith erases the water itself, its physical properties, its movement, its wetness, its transparency. What media-ecological metaphors like Goldsmith's miss is precisely what Timothy Morton writes of in "Ecology as Text, Text as Ecology": "Texts have environments. These environments are made of signs, yet the matter-sign distinction breaks down at a certain point, because one of these environments is *the environment*" (2010, p. 3, emphasis in original). Of course, Morton's own work is invested in troubling the idea of Nature with a capital "N"—his point is that anti-realist metaphors such as Goldsmith's "textual ecosystem" only make sense if we ascribe to a woefully outdated view of a gap between nature and culture. Only by suppressing anti-realist anthropocentric metaphor, by taking media ecology literally (as I suggest in my final chapter), by turning its attentions to things as they are for themselves, can poetry stake out an ethical position in relation to "the real world."

What is a less metaphorical poetry? Suppressing metaphor—at least certain kinds of metaphor—poetry is an avowedly realist venture. In recent years, philosophers, scholars, and poets alike have rekindled interest in realism, most visibly (and contentiously) the Speculative Realist movement. One antecedent to such realism, though, which approaches objects not with anthropocentric metaphors but with a descriptive posture more familiar to the natural sciences may be found in the work of the mid-century French poet Francis Ponge. Ponge is the ideal candidate to present this alternative, since as Bruns writes, Ponge's work exhibits a "careful attention to the things of the world and a kind of selflessness and straightforwardness with respect to them—for example, not turning them into metaphors or stand-ins for one's own experience" (2012, p. 88). Though Ponge first received critical attention in 1942 with his first book of poetry *Le Parti Pris de Choses* (*Taking Sides with Things*), his work is strikingly contemporary considering the materialist philosophy coming from Latour, Bennett, Morton, and elsewhere. That first collection features tight, focused descriptive portraits of the lives of quotidian things like rain, snails, and moss, but Ponge's clearest statement of his poetic project appears in a later volume entitled *La Rage De L'Expression*, or *Mute Objects of Expression*. This work, a collection of writings from across several decades of work, features a handful of extended, self-referential works that meditate both on the objects Ponge is studying and the methods with which he is studying them, intending to "[a]ccept the challenge things offer to language" (2008, p. 37). Accepting that, in his words, certain objects "defy language," means putting knowledge first and poetry second: "The point is knowing whether you wish to make a poem or comprehend an object" (Ponge 2008, p. 4). Ponge opts to emphasize the latter. But this method of comprehending an object demands an ethical position of mutuality or reciprocity toward that object, or what Ponge later calls "co-nascence." By unpacking this term, we find that not only is the concept of co-nascence central to Ponge's poetic project but it carries wide-ranging implications for contemporary poetics and politics as well, in its use of anthropomorphism to resist anthropocentrism, and in its insistence on a mutual materiality between the object and the poem.

In "The Pine Woods Notebook," Francis Ponge uses the term "co-nascence" to refer to his poetic project approximating the essential reality of the pine forest in written language. He writes, "If we've made our way into the familiarity of these private chambers of nature, and if they were thereby brought to new life in speech, it is not only so we may grasp this sensual pleasure anthropomorphically, but also that a more serious co-nascence may come of it" (2008, p. 90). A more serious co-nascence. In the original French, Ponge uses the word "co-naissance" (2011, p. 94). Translated literally, this means "co-birth." The root word, "naissance," suggests birth, or nascence, and the addition of the prefix "co-" changes the sense to a common, mutual, or reciprocal birth (*OED* n.d.). The English translator of much of Ponge's work, Lee Fahnestock, opts for the admittedly more poetic term, "co-nascence," likely intending to retain some of the wordplay from the original French.[1] Homophonically, "co-naissance" (with a hyphen) is identical to "connaissance" (with an extra "n"), which is French for knowledge, but can also mean "acquaintance" or "awareness." Ponge is undoubtedly familiar of the various senses of the term, considering his repeated references to the *Littré*, an etymological dictionary compiled by Emile Littré in 1863. Etymologically speaking, the term "nascent" comes from the same root as "genital," which carries the senses of creation and reproduction (*OED* n.d.). Co-nascence thus etymologically evokes the sense of a common or mutual birth, which is perhaps a birth into knowledge, or co-creation or reproduction.

But what elements share in this common birth? Namely, the object and the poet, both born into language in the record of their meeting, which is the poem. Later in "The Pine Woods Notebook," Ponge uses the root word, "naissance," or birth, in a passage that gives an indication of the parties sharing in co-nascence. He writes, "The birth [naissance] in the human world of the simplest things, their accession by the spirit of man, the acquisition of corresponding qualities—a new world in which men and things together will enjoy harmonious relations: that is my poetic and political goal" (2008, p. 122). Harmony, in this sense, evokes an absence of hierarchy, a co-emergence of language and world.[2] By calling for a more

---

[1] In the second volume of his *Seminar*, Jacques Lacan also calls upon this wordplay as *world-play* in a context like Ponge's: "between subject and object there is coaptation, *co-naissance*—a play on words retaining all its force, for the theory of knowledge lies at the heart of any discussion of the relation of man to world. The subject has to place himself in adequation with the thing, in a relation of being to being—the relation of a subjective being, but one that is truly real, truly aware of being, to a being one knows to be" (1988, p. 223). In other words, subjectivity in Lacan's view is not individual but relational.

[2] Especially urgent for Ponge, considering that this text was written during the Nazi occupation of France.

serious co-nascence, Ponge stakes out an ethical position in his poetics whereby subjects and objects are mutually responsible, signaling the breakdown of the subject–object binary in favor of reciprocity, in his endeavor for harmony between humanity and the world.

Ponge's goal, that of "harmonious relations" between humanity and things in the world, may seem utopian. Yet, in a study called *Mimologics*, Gérard Genette tracks just such a utopian tradition in the literary arts in the form of a poetic speculation that he calls "mimology," or "a reflective analogy (imitation) between 'word' and 'thing' that motivates, or justifies, the existence and choice of the former" (1995, p. 5). Unsurprisingly, Genette cites Ponge as a poet whose work exemplifies such poetic speculation, quoting another of Ponge's axioms: "Parti pris de choses égale compte tenu des mots," or "taking side with things equals taking account of words" (quoted in Genette 1995, p. 297). From Genette's perspective, Ponge is a kind of linguistic materialist, who considers words as objects alongside other objects in the world (1995, p. 297). Essentially, Genette defines Ponge's project as a poetics of equivalency, refusing to subordinate the word to the object or the object to the word. Genette's English translator, Thaïs E. Morgan, echoes this ambiguity: "Has Ponge invested his poetics in things (choses) over words (mots), or in words over things, or in both at the same time?" (1995, n. 297). In other words, Ponge's is a poetics that is *less metaphorical*. In place of metaphor, Ponge substitutes a kind of mimetic experiment.

Though both mimesis and metaphor are commonly understood as forms of resemblance, Ponge's affinity for mimesis should not be construed as metaphor by another name. To borrow Stephen Halliwell's (2002) divisions of classical mimesis, Ponge engages in a world-simulating mimesis, rather than a world-reflecting mimesis. World-simulating mimesis is different from a typical understanding of representation. Take photography as an example. Put simply, a photograph represents its object through resemblance. A photograph of a tree looks like a tree. That is world-reflecting mimesis. But world-simulating mimesis is more akin to a photogram, or a cameraless photograph, one of the touchstones of the 1920s avant-garde. To make a photogram, the photographer places object directly on a sheet of photosensitive paper and then exposes it to light, producing a shadowy or negative image of the object. In this way, the photogram does not so much resemble the object, but contains a trace of the object and simulates the physical contact with the object for the viewer. This is essentially how Ponge attempts to bring "mute objects" into (ontological relation with) language (and vice versa), arguing that poetry "produces a play of mirrors that can reveal certain persistently obscure aspects of the object. The reciprocal clash of words, the verbal analogies are one of the means for studying the object in depth" (2008, p. 4). Ponge regularly acknowledges the distortion that language enacts on objects, but hopes, through the concept of co-nascence, to bring objects into language in a way that simulates, rather than reflects, their material qualities.

This materiality is central to Ponge's theory of co-nascence, and it is what puts him in conversation with contemporary materialist philosophy. In an interview with Serge Gavronsky, Ponge says, "I try, in the verbal world, to do something which has as much concrete existence as the objects I describe. Poetry has to be considered, above all, as the art and science of existence" (1977, p. 96). Language, and therefore poetry, has a material existence. Poems, like objects, are made of matter. So, for that matter, are poets. The encounter between the poet and the object produces a third object: the poem. Yet, for Ponge, to describe an object in language does not exhaust that object's reality. In fact, the project of co-nascence seems to be an exchange of places: the poet attempts to realize the experience of the object. Or, to put it in terms of metaphor: rather than using objects as metaphors for human emotions and experiences (which we might call the anthropocentric approach), Ponge uses human emotions and experiences as metaphors for an object's experience (the anthropomorphic approach). Ponge's co-nascence, then, does not do away with metaphor altogether, but rather inverts metaphor.

One exemplary passage comes from Ponge's "Notes for a Bird." He writes,

> The bird takes comfort in its feathers. It is like a man who would never part with his comforter and down pillows, who carries them around on his back and could at any moment nestle down in them ... Put yourself in the place of this stump-armed gimp with pockmarked, fettered legs, obliged to hop along in order to walk, or to haul about an enormous belly. Fortunately, a very mobile neck, as much for guiding the beak toward the snapping up of prey as for cocking the ear to warnings of impending danger, since in any event he can find refuge only in flight—beady-eyed, alert for both prey and predator, forever on the lookout—heart and wings aflutter. (2008, pp. 21–22)

As we can see from the above passage, Ponge not only anthropomorphizes the bird by comparing it to a man with a comforter but also invites the reader to imagine the physical experience of the bird. The object, the bird, takes primary status, to the extent that the above passage is hardly recognizable as a poem. Ponge has an answer for this: "I hardly care whether someone chooses to call the outcome a poem. As for me, the slightest hint of poetic droning simply reminds me that I'm slipping back into that old merry-go-round and need to boot myself off" (2008, p. 4). That "merry-go-round," for Ponge seems to be a poetics that denies its materiality, that imagines the poet, the subject, above and outside, rather than implicated in the material contact between poet and object.

Ponge attempts to achieve "a more serious co-nascence" by anthropomorphizing objects as a way of uncovering their qualities. This anthropomorphism insists that language has the capacity to produce such real knowledge of objects. Ponge's affinity for anthropomorphism is echoed in Jane Bennett's *Vibrant Matter*. Drawing on Darwin's tendency to anthropomorphize worms, Bennett writes, "A touch of anthropomorphism, then, can catalyze a sensibility that finds a world filled not with ontologically distinct categories of beings (subjects and objects) but with variously composed materialities" (2010, p. 99). As Bennett and Ponge would certainly agree, anthropomorphism (a form of metaphor) is not an end in itself but a mere catalyst, and this anthropomorphism is only effective if leveraged against anthropocentrism. The implication here is that humanity's sense of subject is a grammatical construction, rather than an ontological reality, and that we (poets, critics) should pursue what these "variously composed materialities" have in common, rather than what justifies humanity's dominion over nature.[3] Similarly, in *Alien Phenomenology, or What It's Like to Be a Thing*, Ian Bogost proposes the term "metaphorism" to describe the way objects relate to each other, even without the influence of humans. He writes, "what if we deployed metaphor itself as a way to grasp alien objects' perceptions of one another" (2012, p. 67).

---

[3] In a discussion of Ponge's ambivalent relationship to anthropomorphism, Barbara Johnson writes, "To eliminate anthropomorphism would in essence be to eliminate language itself: what other species uses it?" (2008, p. 32). In fact, many poets have experimented with nonsemantic or, as Steve McCaffery (2001) terms it, "protosemantic" poetry, though the degree to which a poem consisting of words or sounds or even recontextualized objects successfully "eliminates language" is subject to debate, given that such works—even in oppositional terms—define themselves in relation to language.

Metaphor, for Bogost as for Ponge, is a way for thinkers to explore "what it's like" to experience the world as a nonhuman object.

Some may object to what appears to be the apolitical nature of such materialist musings, despite its explicit engagement with power relationships, given that the outcomes are less clearly defined than those of traditional critique. What is to be gained by attributing agency to nonhumans? What does such a materialist posture as co-nascence have to do with the urgent political issues of our day—climate change, for example? For this is precisely what Ponge, Bennett, and Bogost are suggesting. Ponge writes, "The object is always more important, more interesting, more capable (full of rights): it has no duty whatsoever toward me, it is I who am obliged to it" (2008, p. 4). What is at stake if, for example, we began to acknowledge the rights, whole range of entities, most of which are, in fact, not human? This is already happening to some degree in our legal system. In many cities around the U.S., lawyers are suing for rights on behalf of animals such as chimpanzees. Peter Singer, the renowned ethicist, continues to advance the term "speciesism," as an analog to racism or sexism, to indict the viewpoint of human supremacy over nonhumans (1990, p. 6). And, even more aptly in context of this project given the origin of paper as wood pulp, Christopher Stone (2010) argues that even trees should be recognized as in possession of some legal rights.

These conditions are, in part, the context for a contemporary poetic work by Yedda Morrison, entitled *Darkness*. With *Darkness*, Morrison takes the Signet Classics edition of Joseph Conrad's *Heart of Darkness* and erases all references to humanity and human culture. Morrison's erasure occasionally leaves whole pages blank except for phrases like "river- / light," giving the reader the uneasy sense of "discovering" nature (2012, p. 18). Yet what is discovered is not nature but its index. Taking references to humanity out of the text cannot fully remove humanity from the text: "river" is not the river's word for river but rather the deformation of a river into human language. Yet, Morrison's erasures seem to be searching for both the literal and conceptual "ground," the place at which language adheres to the natural world. Poetic experiments of this kind enact what Ponge calls the poet's obligation to the object.

These moves have consequences for literary studies as well, and they have already contributed to what some have called the decline of cultural studies. Alex Galloway offers this incendiary remark from a colleague, who said, "Do we really need another analysis of how a cultural representation does symbolic violence to a marginal group?" (2012, p. 120). Galloway is not suggesting that those who work in cultural studies be silenced, but he, along with Bennett and Bogost, have called into question the efficacy of such approaches at effecting political change. To borrow Ponge's phrase, cultural studies' version of critique seems to be that merry-go-round, and these thinkers are attempting to persuade us to boot ourselves off. The consequences of this shift are still in formation. But Ponge's theory of co-nascence does not presume a zero-sum game in which recognizing rights for nonhumans means denying them to humans. Rather, Ponge proposes a poetics that refuses to instrumentalize and exploit the world through metaphor, and instead attempts to deploy anthropomorphic metaphor as a means of acquiring knowledge about the world, for the purposes of bringing about ethical interactions with the world. The objects of Ponge's co-nascence may be considered "common." But they are not only common because they are quotidian; rather, they are common because of what the objects and the poem and the poet have *in* common: physical properties, and, I will argue, agency.

This project subscribes to the Actor-Network Theory view of agency as "that which makes or promotes a difference in another entity or in a network" (Sayes 2014, p. 141). But to say that objects, poems, and poets have agency in common does not mean that each individual entity is possessed of independent agency but rather that these entities are participants in a pluralized form of agency (Sayes 2014, p. 144). The associations between and among objects, poets, and poems are too complex, I contend, to ascribe to any or all the ability to act totally independently. One of the central lessons of Francis Ponge's poetry, anticipating contemporary media theory, is that no thing or object can be considered in isolation, but rather in context of its media-material networks: in Ponge's case, the relationship between things, the language used to describe them, and the point at which the ability of language to facilitate description breaks down.

Though his work is rooted in the Linguistic Turn of the mid-twentieth century, Ponge's posture toward language anticipates Slavoj Žižek's recent call to trace the emergence of a "neutral medium of designation":

> 'discursive materialism' relies on the so-called 'linguistic turn' in philosophy which emphasizes how language is not a neutral medium of designation, but a practice embedded in a life world: we do things with it, accomplish specific acts ... Is it not time to turn this cliché around: who is it that, today, claims that language is a neutral medium of designation? So perhaps, one should emphasize how language is not a mere moment of the life world, a practice

within it: the true miracle of language is that it can also serve as a neutral medium which just designates conceptual/ideal content. In other words, the true task is not to locate language as a neutral medium within a life-world practice, but to show how, within this life world, a neutral medium of designation can nonetheless emerge. (2013, p. 7)

In some ways, in fact, Ponge's theory of co-nascence is more contemporary than Žižek's neutral medium: Žižek seems to call for a kind of transparent designation in which the medium noiselessly (in the information theory sense) transmits the message, but Ponge's posture is more ontologically neutral regarding the interplay of words and things. Bruns again: "this relation [between words and things] is not simply one of nomination, designation, predication, or description; that is, it is not a relationship of *mediation* linking entities across an ontological divide, but a relationship of proximity, intimacy, and perhaps even identity provided by a shared plane of existence" (2012, p. 81). I take Bruns's reference to mediation to mean mediation conventionally conceived as a hierarchical relationship between incommensurable subjects and objects, not a categorical dismissal of mediation. Ponge's poetics, then, take up a position of equivalency that regards words and things as equally real, that words are a literal (in many senses) subset of things, rather than a conceptual container for ideas, that language is not the sole poetic medium, but that the true sphere of poetic investigation is the friction between word and world.[4]

In recent years, a poetic tradition in the vein of Ponge's co-nascence has emerged, a poetics that further literalizes Ponge's regard for language as a physical object with an increased emphasis on the issue of media. But whereas Ponge's project emphasizes equivalency (words have a non-arbitrary relationship to referents), the new poetics emphasize emergence (media have a non-metaphorical relationship to environments, in that they emerge from said environments). This emphasis on emergence comes in the form of medium reflexivity: the poets I discuss—Susan Howe, Yedda Morrison, and Tan Lin—use appropriation and interactivity to foreground the material properties and modes of composition of their works in a way that subordinates hermeneutics to ontology. Though each of the works discussed exhibit variations in its relationships to critique and

---

[4] Tom Eyers suggests, referring to an interview from 1974 (which he does not directly quote), that the objects of Ponge's work are "ultimately at the service of the rejuvenation of language itself" (2017, p. 61). Yet this is not at all clear in, and even contradicted by, Ponge's writings in the 1940s, as I have suggested above in reference to the concept of *co-naissance*.

anthropomorphism, in essence, the new poetics constitutes a kind of meta-co-nascence: an equivalency between human and nonhuman systems, a speculative poetics founded on attention to the paradoxical friction between the material and linguistic properties of written texts, attempting to consider or speculate on all properties of written texts on the same ontological plane.

New poetics require new forms of reading. What I propose, however, is in fact an anti-reading: emergent poetics as a kind of hermeneutic agnosticism, a rejection of hierarchies concerning the intelligible (linguistic) and supposedly unintelligible (material) properties of cultural production. Emergent poetics supplant a non-literal view of media ecology: I hope to resituate media ecology within and among ecosystems, demonstrating how this theoretical framework, rather than being superimposed upon works of poetry, emerges and propagates from poetry as its source and soil.

Emergent poetics, as I argue, respond to and build upon convergent trends in contemporary literary and cultural studies, media study, and social theory: the turn toward what Eve Sedgwick (2003) has called "reparative reading," the emergence of anthrodecentrism (as distinct from posthumanism) in media theory, and the plurality of agency in Actor-Network Theory.[5] Building on Paul Ricœur's idea of "the hermeneutics of suspicion," Sedgwick coins the term "reparative reading" as an alternative to the prevailing, suspicious "paranoid reading" of institutional critique. Sedgwick suggests that "the methodological centrality of suspicion to current critical practice," and its "privileging of the concept of paranoia" depend too heavily on negative affect and the formulaic unveiling gesture of exposing the institutionalized ideologies lurking within cultural forms (2003, p. 125). In contrast, reparative reading is "additive and accretive ... it wants to assemble and confer plenitude on an object," rather than subordinate the object to the revelation of ideologies lurking behind it, emphasizing neutral or positive affect and pluralities of meaning (Sedgwick 2003, p. 149). In response to Sedgwick, I would argue that the reparative mode is truly *anti-reading*—what passes for "paranoid reading" is in fact a text-processing program with predictable outputs such as (in Sedgwick's words) "parody, denaturalization, demystification, and mocking exposure of the elements and assumptions of a dominant culture," which forecloses on constructive, positive affect (2003, p. 149). Reparative reading, by

---

[5] "Anthrodecentrism": a term which I believe was first used by Matthew T. Segall (2011) on the blog *Footnotes2Plato*, in a post about Graham Harman and Object-Oriented Ontology.

contrast, emphasizes the plurality of an assemblage of materials and forces gathered within an instance of written culture, rather than imposing a unified (reductive) politics on a text.

In contemporary media studies, the ubiquity of digital media has prompted skepticism of so-called paranoid methodologies and given cause to rethink humanity's relationship to "old" or "analog" media as well. Both the structure and function of digital media have prompted a rethinking of McLuhan's view of media as prosthetic, that media function primarily as extensions of the human sensorium. Media theorists such as Mark Hansen (2015) and Jussi Parikka (2015)—representing the two central veins of media theory, networked and material-specific views of media, respectively—have recently proposed more anthrodecentric theories of media. Though their spheres of inquiry diverge, both Hansen and Parikka depart from orthodoxy by advocating for a media theory that is not centered on revealing an ideological set of media effects on human consciousness. Parikka's *A Geology of Media* radically expands the field of media archaeology (tracing the histories of material inscriptions), advocating for "the necessity to analyze media technologies as something that are irreducible to what we think of them or even how we use them" (2015, p. 1). Building on theories of deep time, Parikka's media theory centers on the material importance of elements such as lithium, which he calls "a premediatic media material," the central component that enables the power and functionality of digital media (2015, p. 4). Whereas Parikka interprets media's materiality from the perspective of a geologic past, Hansen rethinks media systems through the lens of the contemporary: "Life in twenty-first-century media networks reveals something that has perhaps always been the case, but that has never been so insistently manifest: agency is *resolutely not* the prerogative of privileged individual actors" since so much of the functionality of digital media occurs at scales to which humans to not have direct control (2015, p. 2). The lessons of digital media fold back on what is conventionally known as "analog" storage media: the pluralization of agency demands a rethinking of the anthropocentrism of historical media studies. As an alternative, Hansen advocates for a view of "*non-prosthetic* technical mediation," a perspective which is essentially neutral: "absolutely no privilege is given to any particular individual or node, to any level or degree of complexity" (2015, p. 2).

Like both reparative reading and anthrodecentric media theory, Actor-Network Theory (or ANT) resists the reductivity of ideological critique by pluralizing agency, which consequently reduces oversimplifications of causality and responsibility. In *Reassembling the Social: An Introduction to Actor-Network Theory*, Bruno Latour (ANT's originator), argues that "Action is not done under the full control of consciousness; action should rather be felt as a node, a knot, and a conglomerate of many surprising sets of agencies that have to be slowly disentangled" (2005, p. 44). In this way, Latour cautions against attributing agency to individuals, considering the assembled, collective nature of action. The dominant methodologies of ANT are simultaneously assembling and disassembling: the conglomerate must be constituted as a sphere of inquiry prior to its disentangling at the hands of the ANT researcher. Crucially, according to Edwin Sayes, "ANT aims to become insensitive to any a priori difference between humans and nonhumans" (2014, p. 145). To sustain this view, ANT expands the idea of agency such that "it catches every entity that makes or promotes a difference in another entity or in a network" (Sayes 2014, p. 141). As a "theory" that attempts to assemble and disentangle a network of human and nonhuman agencies, ANT emphasizes not ideology but methodology in a way that recalls both Sedgwick's view of reparative reading as localized rather than unified and the anthrodecentrism of Parikka's media archaeology and Hansen's systems view of media.

All three of the above trends converge at an acknowledgement of the exhaustion of institutional critique and an emphasis on local methodology rather than grand theory. This project argues that the exhaustion of paranoid criticism warrants emergent readings of contemporary poetic methodologies, refusing polarity, paranoia, and prosthesis. I present the poetic texts discussed below as exemplars because they all undertake to provide alternatives to anthropocentric critique, though the degree to which they remain engaged with critique varies. Ultimately, I do not propose to offer a so-called strong theory—a reductive, one-size-fits-all critical lens. Rather, my view of emergent poetics may be characterized by what Sedgwick calls "weak theory": "there are important phenomenological and theoretical tasks that can be accomplished only through local theories and nonce taxonomies; the potentially innumerable mechanisms of their relation to stronger theories remain matters of art and speculative thought" (2003, p. 145).

This project's three chapters serve as localized case studies in emergent poetics, supported by three central claims, each of which are best illustrated through a paradox, a reflection of the central paradox of emergent poetics: reading as anti-reading. In the first chapter, I explore the implications of a view of media that is non-prosthetic, illustrated by the paradox of telepathic materiality in Susan Howe's *Frolic Architecture* (2010), a long poem composed of collaged archival fragments. I look specifically at how James Welling's photograms, or cameraless photographs, included as illustrations in *Frolic Architecture*, provide a methodological analog to Howe's collage poems. Though I illustrate the limitations of Howe's view of telepathy—communicating with dead authors by engaging with their archives—I suggest that the appropriative character of a photogram-poetics nonetheless provides a template for engaging with a non-prosthetic view of media by refusing to reduce a text to its merely interpretable properties.

In the second chapter, I illustrate how a non-prosthetic view of media resists anthropocentrism, arguing that materiality is anthrodecentric, illustrated by the paradox of nonhuman narrative in Yedda Morrison's *Darkness* (2012). In *Darkness*, Morrison has performed what she calls a biocentric reading of Joseph Conrad's *Heart of Darkness*, meaning that she has erased or "whited-out" all references to humanity from the original text, leaving only references to the natural world. Like Howe's collages, Morrison's disruptive methods foreground the visual and material properties of the print medium, considering them of equal value to the linguistic, representational properties. I point to what might be called reparative impulses in Morrison's text to illustrate the essential contrast between her biocentric method and other forms of erasure poetry. I propose the term "Deep Erasure" to describe the way *Darkness* incorporates the philosophical elements of Deep Ecology to disrupt the hierarchy that places human experience above nonhumans.

Finally, in the third chapter, I argue that materiality is agential, illustrated by the paradox of ambient textuality in Tan Lin's *Heath: Plagiarism / Outsource* (2012). Lin's text is essentially an inversion of the text–context relationship: the contents of the work are constituted from Lin's online textual environment to simulate this environment for the reader. Building on Timothy Morton's writing on the ambient collapse of the distinction between texts and environments, I propose a non-anthropocentric theory of media that equally attributes agency to environments, networks, and individual actors, both human and nonhuman, providing a vision of emergent poetics that engage with the ontological realignments of the twenty-first century.

References

Bennett, Jane. 2010. *Vibrant matter: A political ecology of things*. Durham: Duke University Press.
Bogost, Ian. 2012. *Alien phenomenology, or what it's like to be a thing*. Minneapolis: University of Minnesota Press.
Bruns, Gerald. 2012. *The material of poetry: Sketches for a philosophical poetics*. Athens: University of Georgia Press.
Eyers, Tom. 2017. *Speculative formalism: Literature, theory, and the critical present*. Evanston: Northwestern University Press.
Galloway, Alexander. 2012. *The interface effect*. Cambridge: Polity Press.
Genette, Gérard. 1995. *Mimologics*. Translated by Thaïs E. Morgan. Lincoln: Univeristy of Nebraska Press.
Goldsmith, Kenneth. 2011. *Uncreative writing*. New York: Columbia University Press.
Halliwell, Stephen. 2002. *The aesthetics of mimesis: Ancient texts and modern problems*. Princeton: Princeton University Press.
Hansen, Mark. 2015. *Feed-forward: On the future of twenty-first-century media*. Chicago: University of Chicago Press.
Howe, Susan, and James Welling. 2010. *Frolic architecture*. New York: Grenfell Press.
Lacan, Jacques. 1988. *The seminar of Jacques Lacan, book II: The ego in Freud's theory and in the technique of psychoanalysis, 1954–1955*. Ed. Jacques-Alain Miller, Trans. Sylvana Tomaselli. Cambridge: Cambridge University Press.
Latour, Bruno. 2004. Why has critique run out of steam? From matters of fact to matters of concern. *Critical Inquiry* 30 (2): 225–248. https://jstor.org/stable/10.1086/ci.2004.30.issue-2.
———. 2005. *Reassembling the social: An introduction to actor-network theory*. Oxford: Oxford University Press.
Lin, Tan. 2012. *Heath course pak*. Denver: Counterpath.
McCaffery, Steve. 2001. *Prior to meaning: The protosemantic and poetics*. Evanston: Northwestern University Press.
Morrison, Yedda. 2012. *Darkness*. Los Angeles: Make Now Books.
Morton, Timothy. 2002. Why ambient poetics? Outline for a depthless ecology. *Wordsworth Circle* 33 (1): 52–56. https://jstor.org/stable/i24039901.
———. 2010. Ecology as text, text as ecology. *The Oxford Literary Review* 32 (1): 1–17. https://jstor.org/stable/44030819.
OED (*Oxford English Dictionary*). n.d.. https://www.oed.com. Accessed 27 June 2017.
Parikka, Jussi. 2015. *A geology of media*. Minneapolis: University of Minnesota Press.
Ponge, Francis. 1977. *The sun placed in the abyss, and other texts*. Trans. Serge Gavronsky. New York: Sun.

———. 2008. *Mute objects of expression*. Trans. Lee Fahnestock. Brooklyn: Archipelago Books.
———. 2011. *La rage de l'expression*. Paris: Gallimard.
Sayes, Edwin. 2014. Actor–network theory and methodology: Just what does it mean to say that nonhumans have agency? *Social Studies of Science* 44 (1): 134–149. https://jstor.org/stable/43284223.
Sedgwick, Eve Kosofsky. 2003. *Touching feeling*. Durham: Duke University Press.
Segall, Matthew T. 2011. *Cosmos, anthropos, and theos in Harman, Teilhard, and Whitehead*. Footnotes2Plato. https://footnotes2plato.com/2011/07/12/cosmos-anthropos-and-theos-in-harman-teilhard-and-whitehead. Accessed 4 June 2014.
Singer, Peter. 1990. *Animal liberation*. New York: Random House.
Stone, Christopher D. 2010. *Should trees have standing?: Law, morality, and the environment*. Oxford: Oxford University Press.
Žižek, Slavoj. 2013. *Less than nothing: Hegel in the shadow of dialectical materialism*. New York: Verso.

CHAPTER 2

Photogram as Poetic Method: Susan Howe's Materialist Telepathy

In this chapter, I explore the possibilities for and implications of an emergent poetics in the photographically inflected poetics of Susan Howe's long poem *Frolic Architecture* (2010). This long poem, published as a single volume and collected in *That This* (2010), features several photograms by James Welling. A photogram, or cameraless photograph, is a kind of shadowy contact print made using an object rather than a photographic negative. I ask what Howe's remediation of the method of the photogram, a nineteenth-century medium, offers twenty-first-century poetry. I suggest that Howe sees these photograms as analogous to the accompanying poems in terms of methodology; she employs a kind of photogram-poetics. Howe's photogram-poetics, the cutting and collaging of facsimiles of archival documents to foreground the visual and material qualities of print, echoes Kabbalistic anagrams and Dadaist collages in the way it attributes agency to the collaged print fragments themselves. By foregrounding the printed medium, rather than its "content," Howe resists the conventional hermeneutic impulse toward textual interpretation, instead attempting to conjure the "ghosts" of the texts' authors (which, as I will argue, is one of the limitations of Howe's project). That is, rather than simply pointing to the artifice of the medium—its illusion of transparency—as a way of critiquing printed texts as social constructions, Howe attempts to present a methodological alternative to negative (or "paranoid," in Sedgwick's (2003) phrase) critique. But Howe's

© The Author(s), under exclusive license to Springer Nature
Switzerland AG 2025
T. W. Matteson, *Emergent Poetics*, Modern and Contemporary Poetry and Poetics, https://doi.org/10.1007/978-3-031-70737-7_2

method is limited in that it exchanges one hierarchy for another in her subordination of the printed texts to the ghosts of their authors in her career-long preoccupation with telepathy. Despite the limitations of Howe's own reading of this method, I argue that Howe's photogram-poetics ultimately appropriate the non-prosthetic mediation of the photogram into the medium of print.

2.1 A Gentle Realism

By now, the most recognizable and celebrated aspect of Susan Howe's poetry is her attention to the visual poetics of print-based documents, what Chelsea Jennings has called Howe's "facsimile aesthetic" (2015, p. 660).[1] Howe describes herself as a "gentle reader": the little violence she inflicts on texts—cut, collage, quote—is always for the purpose of probing pluralities of meaning rather than imposing a single interpretation on a given text (2003, p. 61). But perhaps more provocative is her characterization of these gentle readings as an attempt at realism. *The Midnight*, a kind of autobiographical compendium of original and found text illuminates Howe's realist poetics:

> Every mortal has a non-communicating material self—a waistcoat or embroidered doublet folded up, pressed down, re-folded to fit snugly inside. Incommunicado. Words sounding as seen the same moment on paper will always serve as the closest I can come to cross-identification vis-à-vis counterparts in a document universe. I'm only a gentle reader trying to be a realist. Can you hear me? (2003, pp. 60–61)

In the passage above, Howe curiously implies a comparison between folded articles of clothing and printed texts as a way of thinking through the relationship between visual and auditory elements in a text—"Words sounding as seen." Howe's use of the term "non-communicating" seems less an inherent property of "material selves" and more a function of the attitude of the reader, promoting a sense of textual awareness that parallels the intimacy involved in handling someone else's clothing. This is a call to attunement to textual properties typically overlooked, now invoked as a form of direct visual and auditory communication with the author: "Can

---

[1] See, for example, Craig Dworkin's (1996) "'Waging Political Babble': Susan Howe's Visual Prosody and the Politics of Noise" and Alan Golding's (2002) "('Drawings with Words': Susan Howe's Visual Poetics."

you hear me?" For Howe, this gentle realism means tuning into the particularities of the medium, coaxing the "Incommunicado" materiality of print to speak. More accurately, perhaps, we might say that Howe's realist venture constitutes an attempt to become attuned to aspects of media objects that human readers tend to overlook (a rather McLuhanesque argument)—namely, for Howe's purposes, the ontological implications of foregrounding the physical properties of the print medium. But, unlike McLuhan, Howe seeks to blur the boundaries between the "document universe" and the universe of human subjectivity, suggesting that documents themselves possess a kind of agency.

As John Harkey notes, Howe's is a kind of aspirational, rather than absolute, realism. He writes, "Howe's archive-infused spare assemblages record the impingement of a wounding reality, that is, the 'actuality' of history 'in and against' which she speaks of working" (2013, p. 190). Howe seeks to turn the false linearity of documents, the "Great Men" version of history, against itself, intervening at the level of the print medium to work her revisionist history. Howe's work literally cuts into archives to reassemble documents, often foregrounding historical figures conventionally considered "minor." But, Harkey says, Howe's realism may also be construed as a sort of mysticism, a sense of spiritually becoming one with the objects of her poetry:

> Sustained acquaintance with and good faith investigation of something—whether a tree, person, poetic text, or archive—can begin to yield significant knowledge of that thing, not because of mere rational analysis that a mind has projected but because, in a sense, the thing exudes the meanings that are bound up with its strict particularity, its actual material existence. (2013, p. 190)

Howe's realist mysticism ultimately launches a "sustained acquaintance" with the printed texts, with reference to the existence of such texts in an archive; she waits for them to speak to her, a way of recomposing marginal voices in the historical record. Crucially, this method suppresses the traditionally communicative material—the text—in favor of a greater attention to the physicality of the medium: the weight of the ink, the texture of the page, the glue of the binding, marginalia, handwritten inscriptions, scraps of paper or fabric as makeshift bookmarks, the paper's arboreal origins as trees in a forest, qualities that probe the agential force of the book, notebook, or sheaf of paper. Howe is resistant to the interpretive hierarchy that would subordinate materiality to an abstracted "text" or "meaning." In this way, Howe's gentle realism depends upon what I call emergent poetics. Emergent poetics must be understood as a departure from McLuhan's theory of media as "the extensions of man" (the subtitle to his seminal work, *Understanding Media*). Instead, media should be regarded as non-anthropocentric. Media are, in fact, only media-centric: they exist in and of themselves, rather than as channels for human meaning and ideology. To understand media, then, is to approach it ecologically and holistically—to attempt, at least, to account for the ways a given medium resists or exists outside of conventional interpretive paradigms.

Until recently, Howe's work has exhibited a tone of frustration, failure, (often personal) loss, even anger about what she has called "male editorial meddling," the tendency of women writers to have their works either assimilated into a masculinist normative tradition of historical progress or excommunicated from it (2012, p. 159).[2] Howe's most potent, and most familiar, grievance centers on the editorial treatment of Emily Dickinson's work.[3] However, her latest works, those published since 2009, bear a markedly different tone, a more affirmative poetics that places more emphasis on rectification—rather than critique—of patriarchal narratives. In both her recent poetic works and interviews, Howe's posture is less militant, her anger at the patriarchal bent of editing giving way to a sense of wonder at the possibilities of textual intervention. This is not to say that "male editorial meddling" has altogether disappeared but rather that Howe's most recent work is the closest she has come to short-circuiting the masculinist violence of the textual history, and, consequently, represents the nearest she has come to fulfilling her realist aspirations.

Frolic Architecture, the central text of Howe's recent work, was published by Grenfell Press and collected in a trade version called *That This* in 2010. The Grenfell Press edition displays a spare grey cover bearing only the title, *FROLIC ARCHITECTURE*, in all capital letters. In terms of

---

[2] Howe uses the term "anger" to describe her early work in the Paris Review interview and in a talk at the Kelly Writer's House (2010a). Notably, she makes the distinction between her earlier, more polemical works and her current projects. It is my argument that the critical structures that undergirded the polemic of negative critique are no longer a useful or accurate tool for political engagement.

[3] See Howe's *My Emily Dickinson* (2007a), a critical/creative extended essay on the ways in which Dickinson's editors imposed regularized typography on Dickinson's work. See also Lori Emerson's "My Digital Dickinson" (2008), a writing-through of Howe's earlier work with an emphasis on the materiality of Dickinson's poetry.

size, the book is standard US Letter, at 8 ½ inches by 11 inches. The book includes 48 of Howe's poem-collages and 10 photograms by James Welling, which were commissioned for this work. On the title page in the Grenfell edition, Susan Howe and James Welling are both listed as authors. This contrasts with the version of "Frolic Architecture" that appears in *That This* (the trade paper edition), where Welling's name only appears as an attribution on the copyright page and on the rear cover. The discrepancy between Welling's "co-authorship" of *Frolic Architecture* and his contributor status in *That This* obscures the fact that his photograms were commissioned: the fact that *Frolic Architecture* is a collaboration. Unlike the Grenfell printing, the paperback edition of *That This* features a spare white cover, with Howe's name and the title centered on the page, just above the image of a blue square of fabric, frayed a little at the edges. Readers of Howe's work may recognize this image: it appears in *Souls of the Labadie Tract*, as "Fragment of the Wedding Dress of Sarah Pierpont Edwards" (2007b, p. 112). In addition to "Frolic Architecture," *That This* includes a poem-essay entitled "The Disappearance Approach" in memory of Howe's late husband, Peter Hare, a short poem sequence entitled "That This," and a single fragment, listed only as "[untitled]" in the table of contents.

Photograms, or cameraless photographs, are images produced through direct contact between an object and photosensitive paper. This process, which gained currency in the early twentieth century with such notable practitioners as Man Ray and László Moholy-Nagy, produces shadowy, negative images of the object placed on the paper's surface (Laxton 2012, p. 332). But what does the photogram, that touchstone of the 1920s avant-garde, offer to contemporary poetry? Howe's affinity for the visual arts is well-documented, from her beginnings as a painter to her more recent essay on the films of Chris Marker, entitled *Sorting Facts; or, Nineteen Ways of Looking at Marker*. Both Palattella (1995) and Harris (2006) have argued that Howe's early essay "The End of Art" (1974) indicates the influence of abstract painting on the development of Howe's poetic practice. Despite attention to visual art's contribution to Howe's aesthetic, no extended account of the photograms in *Frolic Architecture* yet exists, perhaps due to the text's relatively recent publication, or the fact that Welling, though listed as a co-author in the Grenfell edition, is only credited on the copyright page and the rear cover of the paperback.[4]

Howe's text in *Frolic Architecture* features collaged fragments from the eighteenth-century American preacher Jonathan Edwards' family archives in Yale's Beinecke Rare Book and Manuscript Library. By copying, cutting, and taping together fragments of these texts, particularly Hannah Edwards Wetmore's diary, Howe recomposes clusters and constellations of text, maintaining the original typography, but rendering much of the text illegible. Formally, *Frolic Architecture* expands and modifies Howe's poetic project of intervening in the historical record, through her own process of cut-up and erasure. As with earlier efforts, Howe turns to the archive as the site of historical violence, what she has elsewhere called "a search by an investigator for the point where the crime began" (1989, p. 21). Though Howe seems to have been working in this style in the final section of *Souls of the Labadie Tract*, "Fragment of the Wedding Dress of Sarah Pierpont Edwards," the poems in *Frolic Architecture* deviate visually from Howe's larger collage poems and what others have called "word squares," or arrangements of text in small quadrilateral forms in the center of the page.[5] In *Frolic Architecture*, the collaged fragments cluster in a variety of shapes, sizes, and locations, from the center of the page to the gutter to the margins, whereas her word squares tend to be more geometrically regular and feature typeset, rather than facsimile, text. Despite these deviations from her previous work, this long poem constitutes, for Howe, a definitive statement on her compositional methods: in an interview for *The Paris Review*, Howe says of "Frolic Architecture," "As I moved between computer screen, printer, and copier, scissoring and reattaching words and scraps of letters, I thought, I've never gone as far or felt as free" (2012, p. 158).

Like Howe's texts, James Welling's photograms—composed by painting on clear plastic sheets and creating exposures of the patterns with photographic paper—are "inspired" by the Edwards Archive, according to The Grenfell Press catalog. Since the 1970s, Welling has experimented with a variety of visual media, his work a constellation of abstractions in

---

[4] Additionally, Howe's audio performance collaborations with electronic musician David Grubbs has shifted the critical focus to the sonic qualities of Howe's texts. See, for example, Edward Allen's "'Visible Earshot' The Returning Voice of Susan Howe" (2012).

[5] See Rachel Blau DuPlessis's "'Whowe': On Susan Howe" from *The Pink Guitar: Writing as Feminist Practice* (1990). and Brian Reed's "'Eden or Ebb of the Sea': Susan Howe's Word Squares and Postlinear Poetics" (2004).

painting, photography, and digital methods. Alain Cueff finds in Welling's abstract work "a new way of relating to the enduring quality of the image and the awareness of history," the history of photographic technology, in particular (1999, p. 11). For Cueff, postmodern concerns about representation and reproduction are less relevant to Welling's work than a sense that the modernist project of abstraction is not yet exhausted (1999, p. 11). The photograms included in *Frolic Architecture* exemplify this sentiment: through the abstraction (removal) of representational content and external reference, the photograms reflexively foreground their own material presence. But that presence is always provisional, contingent, at least for Welling, on history. In an interview with Chris Balaschak, Welling says, "One of my earliest revelations about working with a view camera, was that it had a history built into it" (2008, p. 159). From this perspective, cameraless photography might seem as an attempt to short circuit the history of photography as representation (though of course the photographic paper itself has a history built into it). Welling and Howe share this mediahistorical perspective of turning a medium's history against itself: while Welling says, "You have the history of image making always on the surface of any photograph you make," Howe's work, throughout her career, wears on its surface the history of print (2008, p. 159).

If *Frolic Architecture* is the "furthest and freest" of Howe's works, the photograms accompanying the text also deserve greater attention than they have thus far received. The prominence of the photograms in *Frolic Architecture* suggests that Howe sees the photogram as analogous to her poetic methodology.[6] Just as the photogram disrupts the representational function of photography, Howe's photogram-poetics disrupt the legibility of the print medium. For Howe, this method takes the form of a feminist archival intervention. In a passage from *The Europe of Trusts*, Howe writes, "I wish I could tenderly lift from the dark side of history, voices that are anonymous, slighted—inarticulate" (1990, p. 14). In "*The Difficulties* Interview," Howe says, "Women must rectify what Irigaray calls 'this aporia of discourse'" (1989, p. 23). Howe takes this phrase from Irigaray's essay "This Sex Which is Not One"; the line itself reads "This aporia of discourse as to the female sex," interrogating the fraught relationship between the female voice and the "master discourse" (1985, p. 149).

---

[6] Chelsea Jennings makes a similar point in "Susan Howe's Facsimile Aesthetic": "Welling's process mirrors Howe's in that it involves layering and recopying; the prints represent stages of an ongoing process" (2015, p. 681).

Howe hopes to become attuned to the voices of women ignored or erased from the historical record, through a compositional process that Howe regularly terms "telepathy," which for Howe amounts to a sense of contact with deceased authors based on physical interventions at the level of the print medium (this should recall Harkey's allusion to Howe's "realist mysticism"). While this term appears in the title of Howe's recent work—*Spontaneous Particulars: The Telepathy of Archives*—the term "telepathy" appears in the text of several of Howe's previous works and interviews. Howe's reference to telepathic communication, particularly with Hannah Edwards' archives in "Frolic Architecture," conjures the idea of "medium" in both its material and spiritual connotations.

Howe's photogram method weaves together the pseudo-spiritual practice of anagramming, Dadaist collage theory, and the cultural history of the photogram. Or, rather, the photogram itself represents the convergence of the methodologies of anagrams and Dadaist collage. Anagrams are rearrangements of letters in words or phrase to produce another word or phrase; they figured prominently in Kabbalah and other mystical traditions to divine the words of a deity (Eco 1995, p. 28). Dadaist collage, too, is often couched in the language of mysticism, a rearrangement of found texts, objects, or images that reveals "a ghost, like a prophecy, like the voice of a ouija board, like the desperate cry of a reality imprisoned in its own form" (Hugnet 1981, p. 158). As with anagrams, Howe is cutting up and rearranging letters and words, with special attention to their typographical idiosyncrasies, producing new arrangements, new "messages" in a voice not her own (though also not divine, unlike Kabbalistic anagrams). And like Dada collages, Howe's poems in *Frolic Architecture* rearrange found objects—archival documents—as a way of releasing or communicating with their ghostly authors. Crucially, Howe's poetic method is parallel to that of the photogram—the direct contact between an object and a photosensitive surface. The photogram is the ur-medium: rather than *representing* the visual appearance of its subject, the photogram *presents* the ghost or shadow left by the subject when it encountered the photosensitive paper.

Ultimately, the photogram is both a historically specific material phenomenon and, in its simple transfer of an object's trace, a stand-in for the concept of mediation itself (as it was for many in the 1920s avant-garde).[7] This perspective allows us to read Howe's recent work as an intimation

---

[7] See Susan Laxton's "White Shadows: Photograms around 1922" (2012).

toward emergent poetics, a speculative theory founded on attention to the paradoxical friction between the material and linguistic properties of the medium. Howe's preoccupation with telepathic attunement to marginalized female voices in the archives draws attention to the marginal characteristics of the archival documents themselves: their formal, physical makeup, rather than their so-called content.

Will Montgomery (2010) identifies a similar generative friction in Howe's *Melville's Marginalia* and *Pierce-Arrow*: "As in *Melville's Marginalia*, this emphasis on a moment of pure intellection runs alongside a commitment to encountering the book or manuscript as a material object. The writing urges us to read material and immaterial, mediated and immediate, simultaneously" (2010, p. 137). Instead of "material and immaterial, mediated and immediate," I hope to propose a new vocabulary for what Montgomery, and others, sense in Howe's work. I hope to show how Howe's cultivation of an emergent poetics regarding the perceptual experience of media objects causes a flicker effect, not between mediated and immediate (whatever that would be) but between the qualities of the medium that are readily assimilated into a hermeneutic framework and the qualities of the medium that exceed or inhibit the hermeneutic impulse, qualities we might call "sense" and "nonsense," respectively.

The photogram is the ideal medium in which to make this argument. As Chelsea Jennings notes, the facsimile-poems refuse "to distinguish between marks that are linguistic or nonlinguistic, legible or illegible, deliberate or incidental" (2015, p. 667). In *The Birth-mark: Unsettling the Wilderness in American Literary History*, Howe evokes the neutrality of sense and nonsense as "The other of meaning" (1993a, p. 148).[8] This content-neutrality points toward a greater ontological neutrality of the medium as category.

2.2 A Shadow That Is a Shadow Of

Susan Howe's *Frolic Architecture* includes one epigraph and one pseudo-epigraph—the former from Ralph Waldo Emerson and the latter original, a poem-like construction of two couplets that is clearly distinct from the

---

[8] Note the resonance with Maurice Blanchot's phrase "the *other* of all meaning," from *The Space of Literature* (2010, p. 263). Blanchot writes, "Because of ambiguity, nothing has meaning, but everything *seems* infinitely meaningful" (2010, p. 263). Blanchot's idea of ambiguity creates a flicker effect between sense and nonsense that recalls the photogram.

compositional procedure of the ensuing text. From Emerson, Howe includes the line, "Into the beautiful meteor of the snow" (qtd. in Howe, *That* 37). This line, which Howe appropriates from Emerson's address to the Divinity School in Cambridge, gestures to both Howe's own realist aspirations in embrace of materiality and the origin of the phrase "Frolic Architecture." In the passage from which Howe extracted the epigraph, Emerson writes:

> I once heard a preacher who sorely tempted me to say I would go to church no more. Men go, thought I, where they are wont to go, else had no soul entered the temple in the afternoon. A snow-storm was falling around us. The snow-storm was real, the preacher merely spectral, and the eye felt the sad contrast in looking at him, and then out of the window behind him into the beautiful meteor of the snow. (2012, p. 111)

"The snow-storm was real," says Emerson. The contrast between the reality of the snow-storm and the spectrality of the preacher hinges on Emerson's notion of true faith, discussed earlier in this address, which is manifested in its intimacy with the physical world, rather than a rejection of the physical (2012, p. 111). Emerson's reference to a snow-storm also points us to the poem entitled "The Snow-Storm," from which Howe derives her title, *Frolic Architecture*. Emerson's "The Snow-Storm," personifies the north wind as a mason, hard at work building beautiful structures out of snow. The final lines of the poem describe "the mad wind's night-work / The frolic architecture of the snow" (2004, p. 33). Composing her own *Frolic Architecture*, Howe is the north wind, arranging playfully beautiful clusters of others' words in drifts or rivulets down the page. The wind, so often associated with human breath, is a visual artist, echoing Howe's frequent assertion that sound and sight are mutually implicated in her poetry.

The second epigraph (or the first poem) of Howe's own creation in *Frolic Architecture* sits opposite the first of James Welling's photograms and offers a foothold for understanding both the poems to follow and the photograms that accompany them. Howe writes:

> That this book is a history of
> a shadow that is a shadow of
>
> me mystically one in another
> Another another to subserve. (2010, p. 39)

In this brief passage, Howe begins to define the poetic method of the photogram. First, we find that *Frolic Architecture* is a poem concerned with history ("this book is a history"), and as with Howe's earlier work, we can expect this to be an interventionist history, another attempt to "lift from the dark side of history" a voice that has thus far been mute, or muted (1990, p. 14, 2010, p.). Howe's invocation of shadows, however, is a reference not only to a historical absence, but also to the photograms, their shadowy character (like photographic negatives), and their significance to nineteenth and early twentieth-century culture, as a tool for scientific research and the epitome of abstract art, respectively. Each individual photogram, too, contains its own sense of history in the shadow of its subject. Batchen writes, "There is always this prior moment, this something other than itself, to which the photogram ... must continually defer in order to be itself" (2006, p. 33). This indicates "That this book," is, consequently, a meditation on the photogram as "history" itself and constitutes Howe's attempt to remediate the method of the photogram into her poetics.

The final couplet of this pseudo-epigraph defines the relationship between the poet and the other authors whose work she appropriates in the collages to follow. Howe locates her position as author as "me mystically one in another / Another another to subserve" (2010, p. 39). The key here is "one in another," signaling that Howe's poetics is one of inhabitation. Discussing *The Midnight* and *Souls of the Labadie Tract*, Gerald Bruns argues that "Howe's work is a project of self-formation through the appropriation of the writing (and therefore the subjectivity) of others" (2009, p. 28). Crucially, though, this self-formation is not the product of Howe's imitation or pastiche of the authors whose work she appropriates. Bruns continues, "This self-formation is not just metaphorical but is meant to be taken literally, because for Howe the texts that she reads and cites are pneumatic—inhabited by the ghosts of their authors" (2009, p. 28). What are we to make of Bruns's provocative (and problematic) assertion that Howe's poetics of appropriation is founded upon literal, pneumatic inhabitation? The beginning of *Frolic Architecture* intimates that this inhabitation may occur "mystically," but to what degree can we account for this level of mediumship and mysticism? As a point of clarification, Bruns indicates that this mysticism is easier to accept when we account for the instability of subjectivity itself: "Howe is not interested in self-possession but in self-alterity" (2009, p. 29). Howe's self-alterity is one of mutual inhabitation of subject spaces: since subjects form in the realm of language, to be inhabited by a "ghost" is to be inhabited by language. By intervening in another author's written language at the level of the medium, by cutting up and collaging another's printed works, Howe herself becomes a medium.

In addition to the colloquial usage of "literal" (meaning "free from metaphor" or "in reality"), we should read Bruns's insistence on the word "literal" in context of Howe's work, in its etymological sense of "to the letter" (*OED* n.d.). Howe's pneumatic inhabitations hinge on the physicality of the other authors' language, the smallest part of which is the letter. Howe's photogram method resonates with her early interest in anagrams, the rearrangement of letters in words for the purposes of play or mysticism, as a media-historical phenomenon. In *Sorting Facts; or, Nineteen Ways of Looking at Marker*, Howe catalogs the many writers who dabbled in anagrams, from Puritans to post-modernists. She clearly sees herself within the tradition among "North American writers who inherit this feeling for letters as colliding image-objects and divine messages" (2013, p. 49). From this perspective, we can see Howe's photogram-poetics as a kind of meta-anagram, an anagram that functions at the level of the medium, that rearranges not only letters but their mediated, typographic forms as well.

By revisiting the history of the photogram, from its inception in the nineteenth century to its pivotal role in the 1920s avant-garde, we can better understand not only the historical context and precedents of Welling's photograms but also how Howe's self-alterity is grounded in the materiality of the medium. Though most often associated with 1920s Dada anti-art, in the mid-nineteenth century, the photogram was regarded as a specimen for scientific inquiry. The key figures in this era of the history of the photogram are Anna Atkins and William Henry Fox Talbot. Atkins's "cyanotypes"—exposures of British flora made using the photogram technique—served as specimens for scientific inquiry, as a kind of "field guide" to ferns (Laxton 2012, p. 335, n. 4). In the nineteenth century, cameraless photographs were usually referred to as "photogenic drawings" or "shadowgrams"; the term "photogram" was not used regularly until Lázsló Moholy-Nagy coined it in 1925 (Laxton 2012, p. 332). As Susan Laxton writes, the photogram took on renewed significance in the early-twentieth century avant-garde with experiments by Christian Schad, Man Ray, El Lissitzky, and Moholy-Nagy as an unlikely synthesis between photography and abstract painting (2012, p. 332). The photogram of the 1920s amplifies the absolute referentiality associated with the photography of the time, while also importing the idea of a pure, immaterial conceptuality from abstract painting (Laxton 2012, p. 333). Even the name "photogram" carries with it this ambivalence. Etymologically speaking, the word "photogram" is nearly identical to its counterpart, "photograph": both terms refer to writing with light (*OED* n.d.). Whereas the suffix "-graph" often evokes an instrument of production, "-gram" often signals the object produced by that instrument, as in "phonograph"/"phonogram" and "telegraph"/"telegram." Yet, by definition, the photogram is produced through the absence—the abstraction or removal—of the photographic instrument: the camera.[9] The minor morphemic difference between "photograph" and "photogram" captures the uncanny relationship between traditional and cameraless photography and between the subject of a photogram and the shadowy imprint it leaves on the photosensitive paper.

Welling's photograms for *Frolic Architecture* deviate from the traditional compositional process of the photogram, and, consequently, the received interpretation and use value of the photogram as a medium. Rather than simply placing a found object on photographic paper, Welling painted and folded transparent plastic sheets, and then created exposures of the patterns using photosensitive paper. As a parallel to Howe's text-collages, Welling foregrounds the ink-on-paper identity shared by both the printed texts and the photograms. In a sense, Welling's photograms are an even more absolute expression of the abstraction of the photogram, having no recognizable point of reference in the material world. And yet, as with the photograms of the 1850s and the 1920s, the medium of the photogram appears to be touch: the texture of Welling's photograms has a haptic quality that foregrounds the particularities of the physical medium. Welling says, "Since 1998 I've become sensitized to the idea of the photogram as a shadow of the world coexisting with the optical image made by the camera lens" (2004). Welling's use of the word "sensitized" to describe his above realization recalls the photosensitive surface of a photogram. Paradoxically, the critical value of the photogram today is found in the friction these works generate between the abstract or conceptual domain and the concrete: though these photograms often suppress representation, they still serve as a physical record of contact between some

---

[9] To that end, Geoffrey Batchen argues that the photogram is the true foundation for new media, in its existence as a binary technology creating images in the interplay between the presence and absence of light without the intervention of the camera (2006, p. 32).

object—or substance, in the case of Welling's ink photograms—and the photosensitive surface.

This final point, the photogram as a shadowy or illegible representation coupled with a physical trace, is the thread connecting nineteenth-century cyanotypes and twentieth-century photograms to Welling's work and, consequently, Howe's *Frolic Architecture*, which exists entirely of facsimile collages of typeset archival documents. In Howe's photogram-poetics, another author's text is exposed to light (the light of a copier), leaving a kind of shadow on the pages of Howe's book. Methodologically, Howe's collages in *Frolic Architecture* echo the Dadaist Christian Schad's fortuitously named "schadograph" ("shadow-graph") photograms, which he composed by collaging and exposing newsprint and other scraps of paper and fabric (Laxton 2012, p. 333). Like the schadographs, Howe's photogram-poems are made of often-illegible "scraps" from the Edwards archives. Both the schadographs and Howe's poems tend also to be quite small, hardly measuring a square-inch on the page. And in *Frolic Architecture*, Howe's fascination with shadows and shadow-writing is made quite clear by the poem she includes at the beginning of the text— "a shadow that is a shadow of / me" (2010, p. 39) Yet, this "me" of whom Howe speaks, we recall, is "mystically one in another." This self-alterity, to borrow Bruns's phrase, is physicalized in the compositional method of the photogram. Photograms, in Howe's reading of them, are inhabited by the ghost or shadow of their subjects.

The individual poem-clusters in *Frolic Architecture*, composed of seemingly random selections of archival text arranged haphazardly, point to Howe's continued preoccupation with the photogram. Though much of the text is illegible due to Howe's cut-up method, certain words and phrases remain legible, offering clues as to the archival material that caught Howe's interest. In many cases, though, it would require immense effort to identify the actual archival source for Howe's collages. The word fragment "shaddowe" resonates with the shadowy look of the photograms and with Howe's first poem on shadows (2010). On the facing page, the phrase "where shall I find Real" recalls Howe's own aspirations toward realism (2010, p. 47). Later, Howe returns to the qualities of photograms, as the phrase "shadows & things" and the word "distortion" become visible (2010, pp. 62, 71). One phrase is repeated: "itself not so / the light eith" appears twice in the collage on page 59, and again on page 74.

This cryptic phrase suggests the uncanny nature of the photogram in its evocation of both light and alterity—"itself not so." As is evident from the above images, the individual poems in *Frolic Architecture* often feature a focal point of legible text surrounded by a more obscured or fragmented selection. This relationship, between the central text and its textual border mirrors the haloed structure of the photogram: the central text is the subject in focus, while the outer border of text serves as its "shadow." The shadow of a text is another text. Finally, a longer string of phrases, partially obscured: "'Others, not I, are looking'. / akes use of others as a mirror to look at / onscience" (2010, p. 77). The word fragments appear to be "makes" and "conscience." Repeated references to looking and the projection of the self mirrored onto "others" implicates the visual character of the photogram in the project of subject formation that Bruns identifies in Howe's work.

Because of the distorting effects of the collage, it would be nearly impossible to reconstitute many of the original sources from which Howe derives these fragments. Some, however, are more readily identifiable, demonstrating the complex network of voices inhabiting *Frolic Architecture*: the phrase "Haughtiness is always little violence" is legible; the source, James Fordyce's *Sermons to Young Women* (1766). The original reads, "Haughtiness is always little, violence impotent, and peevishness the infirmity of a child" from a sermon entitled "On Female Meekness" (1796, p. 246). Fordyce is likely an antagonist in the poem, given that the ostensible subject is Hannah Edwards Wetmore, a young woman herself and a likely target for Fordyce's sermonizing. Below, nearly obscured and cutting through more illegible text, is the phrase "Fluminaque obliquis cinxit declivia ripis." The source is the *Metamorphoses* of Ovid, in the original Latin, but Henry David Thoreau is present here as well: the phrase appears in the epigraph to Thoreau's *A Week on the Concord and Merrimack Rivers*, which includes the full stanza from Ovid, in Latin and in English (1980).[10] The line Howe includes—"Fluminaque obliquis cinxit declivia ripis"—translates, in the Thoreau epigraph, to "He confined the rivers within their sloping banks" (1980, p. 4). In this case, unlike the above cuttings from the Edwards archives, the source is evident, but the meaning is not. References to "shadows" evoke the photogram, the darkness of history, but why is Howe drawn to this line from Ovid via Thoreau? Perhaps in the production of this text, this collage, we have our answer:

[10] The full epigraph reads, "Fluminaque obliquis cinxit declivia ripis; / Quae diversa locis, partim sorbentur ab ipsa; / In mare perveniunt partim, campoque recepta / Liberioris aquae, pro ripis pulsant" (Thoreau 1980, p. 4).

just as this line flows from Ovid through Thoreau, Howe confines these rivers of text, choosing their paths—a textual erosion. The river carves rock through the centuries; Howe literally carves typographical "rivers" (blank spaces between words that seem to align on the page) through texts with scissors, simulating the geologic temporality of historical documents.

With *Frolic Architecture*'s republication in *That This*, two other texts bring additional clarity to Howe's photogram method. Along with the original text of *Frolic* Architecture, *That This* includes two other works: a poem-essay called "The Disappearance Approach" and a poem sequence entitled "That This." The first section, "The Disappearance Approach" reflects on the unexpected death of Howe's husband, Peter Hare, finding Howe "Starting from nothing with nothing when everything else has been said" (2010, p. 11). This poem-essay's context—Hare's death—puts it in conversation with *Pierce-Arrow* (1999), one of Howe's earlier works, which was composed after the death of Howe's second husband, David von Schlegel. Yet, the tone of *That This* is quite different from these earlier works. As Will Montgomery notes, the prevailing tone of *Pierce-Arrow* is loss and absence (2010, p. 130). In contrast, the tone of "The Disappearance Approach" is less one of loss than of immanence—a sense that Hare (and eventually Hannah Edwards) can communicate with Howe outside of the confines of language. Even in this section, Howe's photogram imagination is evident. She writes, "Do we communicate in mirror languages, through some inherent sense of form, in every respect but touch? Do we ever know each other; know who we really are? Midas, King Midas—is the secret we take away with us—touch" (2010, p. 34).[11] The physicality of touch, the textual/textural imprint, and its consequences, is often the subject of Howe's work, and a reference to the paradoxical interplay between absence and presence in the medium of the photogram.

If the Midas touch turns daughters into statues, the touch of the photogram turns absence into presence, and vice versa. Touch, embodied by the contact between a photogram and its object, has been a generative preoccupation of many an artist photographer. As Howe likely knows, Welling's earliest works were photograms of hands. As Noam Elcott notes,

[11] Here, Howe refers to the Midas of Nicolas Poussin's *Midas Washing at the Source of the Pactolus* (*That* 34). She may also be recalling the version of the Midas myth from Nathaniel Hawthorne's *A Wonder-Book for Girls and Boys*, in which King Midas's blessing of the golden touch turns to a curse when he touches his daughter and she turns to gold.

both Man Ray and László Moholy-Nagy made hand photograms, the latter of whom was "an important influence on Welling" (2008, p. 30). The hand, the locus of physical touch, also carries graphological connotations. As with the Russian Futurists, for Howe, handwriting takes on a mystic quality, a suggestion of our "material selves." Montgomery writes that, with *Pierce-Arrow* and *Melville's Marginalia*, "Howe moves away from the typographical experimentation of works such as *Eikon Basilike* or *Thorow* toward a visual aesthetic that depends on actual reproductions of the books and papers of others" (2010, p. 132). The trend toward actual reproductions finds its limit case in Frolic Architecture, which, except for the two couplets at the beginning, exists exclusively in the form of photographic reproductions of other texts. But this assertion exposes one of the limitations of Howe's own reading of her photogram-poetics and telepathic contact with a human author: she is dealing not with handwritten documents but with typeset and printed ones.[12]

Montgomery finds in this tendency "a new form of visual citation that is distinct in important ways from the modernist tradition of textual citation" (2010, p. 132). In "The Disappearance Approach," Howe begins to account for her visual citationality, writing, "More and more I have the sense of being present at a point of absence where crossing centuries may prove to be like crossing languages" (2010, p. 31). What Howe invokes here is a kind of historical translation, in which, voices from the past are recontextualized in facsimile to be able to speak. Visual citation is precisely this kind of translation. Recalling Howe's realist project as she defines it in *The Midnight*, we should read this visual citation as an attempt at "cross-identification vis-à-vis counterparts in a document universe" (2003, p. 61). To cross centuries through photogram-poems is to attempt to coax the non-communicating material selves of these authors to speak—their handwriting, the texture of the paper on which they wrote, their marginalia, fragments of their clothing, the overlooked materiality of texts and their authors which, as Montgomery notes, "have, in [Howe's] view, not been assimilated or understood by later readers or scholars" (2010, p. 132). *Frolic Architecture* attempts to foreground the abundance of typographical and medialogical qualities in the medium of print that pass largely undetected in conventional modes of reading and writing that are

---

[12] Howe's most recent work, *Spontaneous Particulars: The Telepathy of Archives* does include facsimile reproductions of handwritten texts by Jonathan Edwards, William Carlos Williams, and others.

not easily digested by hermeneutic interpretation.[13] In essence, Howe's text argues not for a wholesale rejection of interpretation but instead invokes emergent poetics: a print text is not a solitary instance of language but a complex assemblage of materiality, society, and history.

For Howe, the aspiring realist, it is not enough to merely foreground the materiality of the texts. Following "Frolic Architecture" is a shorter piece, which is in fact the title poem. "That This" returns us to the form of the pseudo-epigraph with which Howe begins *Frolic Architecture*:

> Day is a type when visible
> objects change then put
>
> on form but the anti-type
> That thing not shadowed. (2010, p. 99)

These couplets continue to probe the poetics of the photogram, as "Day" (light) creates exposures of objects. Can we obtain or access the "thing not shadowed" through the poetic method of the photogram? Howe is willing to entertain the suggestion: the anti-type, anterior to formation, seems to be Howe's aim. In "The Disappearance Approach," she writes, "I'm trying to capture a moment before mirror vision—because when you view objects that lie in front of your eyes as well as others in the distance behind, what you see in the mirror has already been interpreted" (2010, p. 31). To access that which exists prior to interpretation is Howe's priority; the photogram is her method for suppressing the hermeneutic impulse by focusing on the self-referential qualities of the medium.

This assertion is mirrored in the title of this collection: *That This*. The words "that" and "this" are deeply intertwined. In *Frolic Architecture*, "that" is used as a conjunction, as in "That this book is a history of." But "that" is also a pronoun "Denoting a thing or person pointed out or present, or that has just been mentioned" (*OED* n.d.). The blackbird whistling or just after. "This" is also a pronoun, "Indicating a thing or person present or near ... as being nearer than some other" (*OED* n.d.). "That" and "This" are, in a sense, deictic markers that are both synonyms and antonyms. If we read the title, *That This*, as a phrase with a degree of linearity, we pass from "that" to "this," from something near or recently passed to

---

[13] This tendency recalls the Russian Futurists, particularly the example of Alexei Kruchenyk's *zaum* poem "dir bul schyl," which was published as a lithograph of a handwritten work in *Pomade* in 1913 (Janeck 1996).

something nearer. To move nearer, to gain a degree of intimacy, is mirrored in the title of the first work in the collection "The Disappearance Approach." On one hand, "disappearance"—Peter Hare, Hannah Edwards Wetmore, both separated from Howe by death—is an "approach" or method. To enter written language is to cause the author to disappear. But "approach" also denotes "the act of coming nearer" (*OED* n.d.). To come nearer by disappearing is paradoxical, but one that resolves in the binary quality of the photogram, which attests to the presence of an object through the abstraction/removal of that object. The photogram, for Howe, retains its subject's ghost, which can be summoned by attending to the material qualities of the photogram. The medium is the medium.[14]

2.3 Mystic Documentary Telepathy

Howe's work since *That This* allows us to read her photogram-poetics in context of her career-long preoccupation with telepathy. In 2013, New Directions republished Howe's essay on Chris Marker as a poetry pamphlet entitled *Sorting Facts; or, Nineteen Ways of Looking at Marker* (2013),[15] and in 2014 printed a longer work by Howe entitled *Spontaneous Particulars: The Telepathy of Archives*. These works, especially their near-simultaneous publication, shed new light on Howe's poetic process. What unites these works, though they were composed nearly 20 years apart, is their emphasis on visual and photographic media and their repeated references to telepathy. Howe composed the Marker essay in the mid-1990s for publication in an anthology of writings on documentary film, but its republication by New Directions indicates its enduring relevance to Howe's poetics. In fact, the Marker essay includes some of Howe's most definitive statements on her poetics to date. Howe writes, "I work in the poetic documentary form, but I didn't realize it until I tried to find a way to write an essay about two films by Chris Marker" (2013, p. 11). The word "documentary" should be read in two ways—as "factual" and as

---

[14] This tautology signals my departure from McLuhanian media theory. Rather than reducing the medium to a set of effects or phenomenological "extensions," Howe's photogram-poetics invite us to understand media not for what they do to or for humanity but precisely the opposite: the ways in which media resist human instrumentalization, the possibilities for a radically nonhuman agency.

[15] The resonance with Wallace Stevens's "Thirteen Ways of Looking at a Blackbird" is clear; Howe's text, her subject (Chris Marker) and Stevens's poem all share an intense focus on sight and the visible word/world.

"textual"—which are often thought of as oppositional. This apparent tension is essentially subject of the essay. At the beginning of the essay, Howe writes, "Without words what are facts?" but she later concludes, "Compared to facts words are only nets" (2013, pp. 7, 45). Can facts exceed or transcend words? Or letters: "A mark is the face of a fact. A letter is naked matter breaking from form from meaning" (2013, p. 49). Again, though the subject of the essay is ostensibly the filmmaker Chris Marker, the essay quickly turns into a reflection on Howe's own poetics: "I call poetry *factual telepathy*" (2013, p. 7, emphasis in original). Factual telepathy is Howe's call to engage with the fact of words, their material existence, not only their meanings.

As the continuity implied in the grammar of the above line suggests, the Marker essay is neither the first nor the only time Howe references "telepathy." In fact, a closer look at Howe's poetry since the 1990s indicates that telepathy has been constant preoccupation. Etymologically, telepathy is perception over a distance, or remote affection (*OED* n.d.). Connotatively, telepathy implies mind-reading, or immediate or unmediated communication. Writing on *Melville's Marginalia*, Will Montgomery suggests that Howe sees telepathy as a metaphor for the way poetic citationality works, "how one writer's words can be said to inhabit another" (2010, p. 119). And yet, as How's poetry makes clear, her investment in telepathy is deeply entwined with her manipulations of the print medium. Can we conceive of a materialist telepathy? Howe's repeated references to telepathy over several decades indicate that such a conception is precisely what leads Howe to the photogram.

One of Howe's earliest references to telepathy appears in *The Nonconformist's Memorial* in 1993—"The brink or brim of anything from telepathy to poetry" (p. 92). The line is part of a large passage that begins, "One way to write about a loved author would be to follow what trails her followed through words of others," indicating that telepathy was already a well-formed heuristic for Howe's interpretation of marginalia and other medialogical phenomena (1993b, p. 92). The next reference sequentially in Howe's work is the "factual telepathy" line from the Marker essay, which was originally published in 1996. Howe returns to this idea in 1999 with *Pierce-Arrow*, with a reference to "printer's copy modern telepathy," again framing telepathy in context of the physical medium of print (p. 81). In 2007's *Souls of the Labadie Tract*, Howe feels "the telepathic solicitation of innumerable phantoms" in Yale's Sterling Library (p. 14). Later, she says of Jean d'Labadie, "His reach is through language hints; through notes and maps … So it's telepathic though who knows why or in what way," echoing the insights she associates with marginalia in *The Nonconformist's Memorial* (2007a, p. 23). And though the word "telepathy" does not appear in the pages of *That This* or *Frolic Architecture*, the final section of the book includes the following lines: "Is one mind put into another / in us unknown to ourselves," which is the very definition of telepathy (2010, p. 104). These lines echo the opening to *Frolic Architecture*—"me mystically one in another" (2010, p. 39). One in another—these references to inhabitation demonstrate that *That This* and *Frolic Architecture* are deeply invested in the question of telepathy.

With the 2014 publication of *Spontaneous Particulars: The Telepathy of Archives*, Howe continues to demonstrate that telepathy is central to her poetics. She writes, "Often, by chance, via out-of-the-way card catalogs, or through previous web surfing, a particular 'deep' text, or a simple object (bobbin, sampler, scrap of lace) reveals itself *here* at the surface of the visible, by mystic documentary telepathy" (2014, p. 18, emphasis in original). Howe's emphasis on the *here* of telepathy recalls the movement from "that"—distant, just past—to "this"—immanent, immediate, present. Howe originally conceived of *Spontaneous Particulars* as a lecture. Amid quotations and brief essay-prose poems like the one above, *Spontaneous Particulars* includes an abundance of visual reproductions of archival materials from several of Howe's intellectual forebears, including Jonathan Edwards, Noah Webster, Hart Crane, William Carlos Williams, among others. If *Frolic Architecture* is the furthest and freest of Howe's poetry, *Spontaneous Particulars* is the most definitive statement on her poetics. In these pages, Howe's preoccupation with telepathy, her focus on the materiality of print, and her emphasis on facsimile converge.

From *The Nonconformist's Memorial* to *Spontaneous Particulars*, telepathy is central to Howe's own understanding of her poetics. But what is the actual character and substance of this telepathy? The answer to this question returns us to the photogram as Howe's poetic method. As we recall from Bruns's assertion, we should take literally Howe's insistence that "the texts that she reads and cites are pneumatic—inhabited by the ghosts of their authors" (2009, p. 28). But while her repeated invocations of telepathy seem to confirm the above assertion wholesale, Howe's language at other times is often more equivocal regarding literal telepathy. In an interview for *The Paris Review*, Howe says, "I honestly don't think that Hannah [Edwards Wetmore] telepathically spoke to me, but something is odd there. I mean, the material—the fragment, the piece of paper—is all we have to connect with the dead" (2012, p. 158). Howe's association of telepathy with materiality reflects the way she uses the term throughout her poetry. She continues, "There's a level at which words are spirit and paper is skin. That's the fascination of archives. There's still a bodily trace" (2012, p. 158).[16] As the material embodiment of telepathy, for Howe, the photogram functions based on the simultaneous flicker between immateriality and materiality, founded upon the constitutive absence signaled by the physical trace. To be attuned to these absences, to refuse the conventional methods of reading and writing that suppress these traces, is Howe's attempt at a gentle realism. This is realism that insists that a mark of ink in a margin or a fragment of a wedding dress can be more evocative than the supposed "content" of a work, allowing Howe to reach, to attempt to touch the ghost of Hannah Edwards Wetmore.

Howe's invocation of the bodily trace should immediately recall the photograms from *Frolic Architecture*. Yet, a tension remains between Welling's photographs and Howe's photogram-poems, a tension that illuminates one of the deepest flaws in Howe's photogram-poetics. Whereas Welling's photographs refer only to themselves, their abstract imagery and their haptic qualities, Howe's telepathic aspirations suggest that her photogram-poems continue to point to a world outside themselves. Howe's flawed attempt at summoning the dead suggests that she is still far more grounded in the anagram, rather than the photogram. Yet, this flaw should not obscure Howe's simple but profound discovery. Her work reveals that conventional modes of reading systematically silence the very material agencies that can communicate so richly across the centuries. The question that the photograms ask is not, then, how to conjure Hannah Edwards Wetmore from the scraps of her diary, though Howe does, at times, seem focused on opening a mystical communication. For Howe, "mystic documentary telepathy" is always provisional, contingent on the materiality of the archive, and not an absolute. The point is to try—"to reach is to touch" (2014, p. 60). In this way, as I hope to show, the limits of the project of *Frolic Architecture* are to be found not its illusory attempts at literal telepathy, or somehow summoning the dead, but rather the difficulty of exorcising from the printed medium its inhabiting ghosts: the

---

[16] Howe's suggestion that paper and words literally, rather than metaphorically, become skin and spirit recalls the Catholic doctrine of transubstantiation. The Catholic Church teaches that during the sacrament of the Eucharist, the bread and wine are not mere symbols of Christ's body and blood but that they become in reality the body and blood of Christ.

traces of its authors, readers, archivists, and its material origins and physical properties.[17]

2.4 The Ghost in the Archive

Howe's recent work, none more than *Spontaneous Particulars*, indicates that she is intensely focused on the idea of the printed medium as it exists within the confines of an archive. She says,

> As they evolve, electronic technologies are radically transforming the way we read, write, and remember. The nature of archival research is in flux: we need to see and touch objects and documents; now we often merely view the same material on a computer screen—digitally, virtually, etc. While I realize that these technologies offer new and often thrilling possibilities for artists and scholars, *Spontaneous Particulars: The Telepathy of Archives*, is a collaged swan song for the old ways. (2014, p. 9)

Despite the nostalgic undertones of the above passage, Howe is no luddite. As she states in her interview with *The Paris Review*, the possibilities afforded to her by the transition to digital technologies created the conditions for one of her most successful works to date. Howe's anxieties seem to stem, rather, from her concerns that digital media operate on a level that does not extend human sensory experience.[18] Howe may see the digitization of archives as an impediment to her realist project, given her focus on the materiality of textual artifacts, a characteristic troubled by the increase in the digitization, particularly the digitization of the archives.

In *The Shape of the Signifier: 1967 to the End of History*, Walter Benn Michaels (2006) raises some objection to Howe's emphasis on materiality. Focusing on Howe's discussion of Emily Dickinson in *The Birth-mark*, Michaels argues that Howe's emphasis on the immediacy of facsimiles of Dickinson's work is contradictory. He points out that a facsimile, like an

---

[17] Though I do not have space for it here, an exploration of the resonance between Walt Whitman's "Whoever You Are Holding Me Now in Hand" and Howe's materialist telepathy may be warranted, given the former's reflection on the poem or the book as a physical presence or embodiment of the absent poet.

[18] Mark Hansen's *Feed-Forward: On the Future of Twenty-First-Century Media* argues that so-called new media merely reveal what has always been the case: "humans must rely on technologies to perform operations to which they have absolutely no direct access whatsoever and that correlate to no already existent human faculty or capacity" (5).

edition, is a reproduction of some, but not all, of a given text's qualities: that is, a facsimile is not an identical object to the original but a reproduction of its visuality (2006, p. 5). Michaels invokes the above distinction to—perhaps rightly—identify inconsistencies in Susan Howe's theory of textual materiality, writing, "Sometimes Howe understands the mark or blank as a form of signification—the expression of an 'athematic compositional intention'; sometimes she turns the mark into a 'trace' that records or reflects a body rather than representing meaning; and sometimes, when the mark becomes 'gibberish,' even what it reflects is rendered irrelevant" (2006, p. 18). These apparent inconsistencies exist in both Howe's reading of Dickinson's work and in her own compositional efforts involving facsimiles.

Yet Michaels goes astray when he attempts to argue that a text cannot be reduced to its materiality. He insists that if a text is only its material or physical qualities, "it ceases to be something that can be edited and thus ceases to be a text at all" (2006, p. 5). In "Susan Howe's Facsimile Aesthetic," Chelsea Jennings attempts to rebut the above claim:

> In Michaels's rendering, the linguistic text must be totally dissociable from the material object or else equivalent to it; however, in reducing textuality to this binary, Michaels neglects visuality—the facsimile's privileged terrain. The facsimile calls attention to the complex relationship between text, visuality, and materiality: text is necessarily visual, and visual features are necessarily material, but the material exceeds the visual, just as the visual exceeds the textual. (2015, p. 667)

Jennings is not quite correct when she argues that "Michaels neglects visuality." In fact, Michaels's argument simply conflates visuality and materiality: "The purely material, in other words, is everything that can be seen by the reader" (2006, p. 6). Jennings is correct, however, to point out that both visuality and textuality depend upon materiality. This is the central argument against Michaels's anti-materialist textuality: unlike materiality, the visual and the textual are interpretive categories and are essentially anthropocentric—to be seen with human eyes and to be interpreted by human consciousness. Materiality, however, must be anthro*de*centric (neutral or non-prosthetic, not an extension of the human sensorium), and this is the central discovery of Howe's photogram-poetics: as Jennings writes, Howe "refus[es] to distinguish between marks that are linguistic or nonlinguistic, legible or illegible, deliberate or incidental" (2015, p. 667).

Though Howe's concerns with the materiality of printed texts in an archive are germane to contemporary debates, any reference to invoking material presence, telepathy, and pneumatic inhabitation is decidedly outside the mainstream of media theory. Yet, the ghostly nature of Howe's collaged conjurings in her photogram-poems coincide with Sven Spieker's discussion of the uncanniness of archives:

> a return of a purloined file is indexed by a sense of fright and unease. When files return to take their place in an archive we think of as being complete—with every record in its appointed place, fully indexed and accounted for—the modernist project of reality-founded rationality and order collapses: the archive becomes literally a haunted place. (2008, p. 4)

In his telling of the history of archivism, Spieker notes that the avant-garde of the early twentieth century called into question the indexical nature of the archives—a document's ability to point to its origin in another time and place—that marked the archival aspirations of the nineteenth century. Troubling the telepathic nature of Howe's archival wanderings is Spieker's characterization of the Dadaist collages as "a form of archivization, an appeal to the fragmentary presence of material objects without regard for past or future" (2008, p. 8). It is here that the Dadaist aspirations and Howe's own collaged archivism diverge. Spieker argues that Dadaist collages represent what Heidegger called *Entbergen*, or revealing: "Unlike poiesis, which implies a direct shift from absence to presence, *Entbergen* uncovers and transforms what is already present yet invisible" (2008, p. 9). In collage, *Entbergen*'s revelatory capacity functions not based on similitude with reality, but rather, by removing all semblance of similitude from the image or images, calling forth qualities of the image that had been obscured by the eye's interpretive gaze. It is clear from Howe's writing in *That This*, though, that her project at least in part focused on rendering present that which is absent—Peter Hare, Hannah Edwards Wetmore. In this way, Howe still seems to be grounded in the nineteenth-century conception of the archive, which Spieker characterizes as the idea that "a record's evidentiary power is a reflection of its origin in a place other than the archive that preserves it" (2008, p. 6). In the archives, Howe's attention is called away from the printed texts before her, her method of composition in collaging these texts amounting to an attempt to reach the author behind the document, outside the archive, what Howe has called "mystic documentary telepathy."

Yet Howe's methods are often at cross purposes with her stated goal of telepathic communication, in particular her failure to include any handwritten manuscripts, which may more readily call to mind the gesture of the body that composed them. Indeed, through Howe's sustained examination, texts in archive seem to take on an agency of their own, rather than embodying or conjuring their authors. Her methods, it seems, are more in line with a kind of animist textual materialism. In *Reading the Illegible*, Craig Dworkin offers an account of Howe's materialist leanings, informed by Claude Shannon's information theory and Michel Serres's notion of the "parasite." Dworkin argues that the unconventional arrangements of text in Howe's poetry "draw attention to the *printer's* art: struck and cut type, the leading and the set of line" (2003, p. 41). Dworkin also notes a recurring motif of Howe's, that of archive-as-forest. The arboreal origins of the print archive are not metaphorical but literal: Dworkin invokes "what Jerome McGann has insightfully read as a reference to 'the material origins' of the page in forests which no longer exist" (2003, p. 43). By attending to the printers, typesetters, and even forestry companies and paper mills that precede a print-based text, Dworkin demonstrates that, in Howe's emphasis on materiality, aspects of the text that would conventionally be read as "noise" are in fact constitutive of the text and inextricable from its meaning-making apparatus (2003, p. 43).

Dworkin's reading of Howe's materialism is modified slightly by his more recent work, *No Medium*, and its affinity with the media theory of Lisa Gitelman (2008). Dworkin's thesis in *No Medium* is that the singular "medium" is a misnomer: "No single medium can be apprehended in isolation … media (always necessarily multiple) only become legible because they are not things, but rather activities: commercial, communicative, and, always, interpretive" (2013, p. 28). In *Always Already New: Media, History, and the Data of Culture*, Gitelman, while not dogmatic about suppressing the singular "medium," similarly insists on the relational aspects of media within "social, economic, and material relationships" (2008, p. 7). The kind of network that Dworkin and Gitelman point to as the true nature of the medium, a network of complex forces and agencies, might from the perspective of Howe's archival intervention be seen as the "ghosts" that lurk just behind the physical medium itself.

Rather than reducing a medium to the sum of its parts and its production, to its ghosts, however, Howe's method of intervening at a physical level in her photogram-poems might exorcise, rather than conjure, these ghosts. Before we can consider this potential, though, we should ask, what kind of archive is a photogram? From the history of the photogram given above, we know that the historical significance of the photogram essentially parallels that of the archives themselves. Consider Spieker's characterization: "Archives do not record experience so much as its absence; they mark the point where an experience is missing from its proper place, and what is returned to us in an archive may well be something we never possessed in the first place" (2008, p. 3). In the nineteenth century, photograms, like archives, were regarded for their status as "evidence" of a subject or point of origin located somewhere other than the final photogram. And Dadaist photograms, like the Dadaist collages as Spieker notes, represent attempts to turn archival logic on its head. In this way, we might see Welling's photographs in *Frolic Architecture* as the Dadaist archive *par excellence*. By removing the camera, by suppressing all content but the abstract textures and folds of the ink on the transparent sheeting, Welling's photographs undertake to produce a kind of Heideggerian *Entbergen* to which the Dadaist collages could only aspire.

To consider Howe's photogram-poems as archives, we need to understand Howe's relationship to the limit case of the archive of linguistic meaning: the letter. As discussed earlier, Howe's photogram-poetics is informed by her interest in anagrams, the dividing and rearranging of letters in a word as play or divination. Anagrams play at the preeminent storage medium of linguistic meaning: the word. The rearrangement of the letters in a word, then, may also be seen as an attempt to purge the word of its denotative content, to reduce it to its phonemic or graphemic parts (in a departure from its use in Kabbalah as a form of divine revelation). "A letter is naked matter breaking from form from meaning," Howe writes (2013, p. 49). This is a vast undertaking, given the deep relationship between meaning—and its primary endpoint in the mind—and alphabetic writing. In a sense, Howe's theory of anagrams would have us disassociate the printed word from a commonplace understanding of what it means to be human. Brian Rotman's *Becoming Beside Ourselves* has recently characterized "Mind, *nous, psyche*" as "media effects of the alphabet, hypostatized entities, ghosts that emerged from the writing of 'I' in the sixth century BCE within the respective Jewish and Greek deployments of alphabetic writing, born at a point when the medium had become naturalized, the effects of written mediation invisible" (2008, p. xxxiii). Rotman's argument hinges on the absence of bodily gesture in written language, facilitating the theories of ideal "mind" that presage the Cartesian mind-body split, arising out of Ancient Hebrew and Greek textual traditions.

His insistence that self-reference in writing gave rise to our concept of "mind" should color our reading of Howe's interest in anagrams. Specifically, by rendering the effects of written mediation visible, by denaturalizing writing, anagrams have the potential to disrupt the ghostly presences that haunt the medium.

What happens when Howe turns her attention from anagrams to archives? In a sense, we might see the collaged fragments—the half-words, the orphaned serifs—of the photogram-poems *Frolic Architecture* as naked matter attempting to break from the form, from the meaning-making apparatus of the archive. The decontextualized fragments that impressed themselves into Howe's vision and onto the page, by chance or choice and a Canon copier, foreground the physicality of these archival documents while also resisting reference and cataloging. From this perspective, the photogram-poems recall Howe's reference to "cross-identification" in *The Midnight*: while these archival documents no longer correspond to any accessible record, they approach Howe's inclination to reconcile the media-perceptual realm with physical reality. By rendering the media effects of archives—their hermeneutic impulse, the false linearity of historical accounts—visible Howe attempts to exorcise the ghosts of patriarchy, what Irigaray calls the "master discourse" (1985, p. 149).

The degree to which Howe succeeds in this attempt is suspect. After all, Howe's readers, as attuned to the visual aspects of the work as they may be, cannot help but surrender to the hermeneutic impulse when faced with the fragments of text. Readers, in a sense, surrender to their own faculties of pattern recognition, looking for repeated words—"light," "shaddowe," "Real." Additionally, Howe seems to have exchanged one category of ghosts for another: instead of being haunted by patriarchy and its demons, Howe's photogram-poems are haunted by the more benign, but still troubling, archival ghost of Hannah Edwards Wetmore, or at least the media effects of her diary's self-referentiality. In her appeals to telepathy, Howe preserves, rather than expunges, the residual impression of the singular mind, in Rotman's terms, from which these diary fragments spring.

But Howe's interest in telepathy, though it perpetuates the fiction of an author standing just behind her text, contains an inkling of truth. As we know from *The Midnight*, Howe's poetic project should be characterized as a realist venture. *Spontaneous Particulars*, too, evokes realist inquiry, with lines like "Things-in-themselves and things-as-they-are-for-us" (18). Howe's poetics are embodied by the photogram, of which Geoffrey Batchen writes, "Here object and image, reality and representation, come face to face, literally touching each other" (2014, p. 32). Her photogram method is thus an attempt to reconcile the latter ("Things-for-us") with the former ("Things-in-themselves"). What is ultimately at stake here, then, beyond questions of telepathy, beyond the apparent paradox of immateriality and materiality, is the question of emergence. Though, by definition, telepathy typically denotes unmediated communication between minds, we have seen that Howe's telepathy is materially grounded in the archive. This suggests that, rather than entertaining a simplistic notion of unmediated or immediate communication, Howe's telepathic aspirations are overshadowed by a posture of emergence *toward* the medium by attempting to approach all properties equally.

Howe's photogram method at least has the potential to resist the tendency of humans to subordinate media objects—which they perceive as existing for their exclusive consumption, to preserve and perpetuate human narratives—by imagin(in)g a poetry in which the poet is but one of a chorus of agencies involved in the production of new texts. One basic medialogical lesson of the photogram, then, is that photography is resolutely not a visual medium. Rather, photography is a *physical* medium, which tends to be interpreted using a visual rubric, to isolate easily assimilable visual qualities to the total neglect of any nonvisual qualities. By the same token, we might begin to rethink what we mean by the word "text." Contrary to what Walter Benn Michaels and others have suggested, a text cannot be abstracted from its material forms. The remediation of this logic into poetics demonstrates the necessity of an emergent theory of textuality, which attempts to assign equal importance to a full range of medialogical qualities.

2.5 Rien négligé

I close with a final image from Howe's *That This*, another collaged photogram-poem that was not originally included in *Frolic Architecture* and is listed as "[untitled]" in the table of contents. The words, taken from a text about the painter Nicolas Poussin, close Howe's text with a cryptic phrase, attributed to Poussin himself: "Je n'ai rien négligé" ("I have neglected nothing") (Stokes 1992, p. 120). The clipping of text that contains this phrase is overlaid with another clipping from the same passage in the biography; the way this second clipping is superimposed on the first, the angle of the cuts, forms a faint X or cruciform on the page, a half-hearted or incomplete attempt to cancel the visible text.

Regarding the text itself, how are we to read Howe's visual citation of Poussin's declaration, "I have neglected nothing"? Is Howe appropriating this text to gesture to the completeness of her project? To say, in a sense, that her archival wanderings constitute a comprehensive portrait of her subject? Perhaps. But that reading itself neglects the visual arrangement on the page and the faint cancellation of the collaged arrangement. We might instead read the word "nothing," not as "I have not neglected any thing," but rather "I have neglected *nothingness*." In a sense, Howe's photogram method has been devoted to revealing (*Entbergen*) the neglected "nothingness" of the print medium, as her collages foreground the invisible characteristics of the medium that are subsumed beneath its more easily interpretable qualities.

Such an attentiveness to nothingness, the irrational (or maybe subrational) materiality of the medium, recalls nothing so much as two of Howe's poetic ancestors: Emily Dickinson, whose envelope poems were recently collected in a facsimile edition called *The Gorgeous Nothings*, and Wallace Stevens, whose poem "The Snow Man" speaks of "Nothing that is not there and the nothing that is" (1990, p. 9). These poets were acutely aware of the problems of interpretation, their poetics often focused on that which exceeds the bounds of hermeneutic interpretation.[19] On the first page of "The Disappearance Approach," the first section in *That This*, Howe writes of "Starting from nothing with nothing when everything else has been said" (2010b, p. 11). Howe's photogram-poetics attempts to speak of nothing, the constitutive nothingness of loss and grief that points her toward the unsaid, the unheard messages left behind in ephemera: in print.

Howe, ever a scholar-poet, leaves this valediction— "Je n'ai rien négligé"—as a challenge to her readers to become attuned to the "neglected nothing," to resist the hermeneutic approach that seeks totality and closure, to the neglect of shadows, the imperceptible or uninterpretable qualities of the medium. The personal grief of the loss of a loved one is thus juxtaposed with a sense of loss provoked by the systematic silencing and subordination perpetrated on the unassimilable qualities of archival documents by the hermeneutic impulse that narrativizes and circumscribes. The lesson of Howe' photogram method is, at last, a theory of textuality that is not centered on the human mind but is an advocacy for a radical neutrality between the (humanly) perceptible and imperceptible qualities of the medium.

---

[19] See Howe's introduction to *The Birth-mark: Unsettling the Wilderness in American Literary History* (1993a).

References

Allen, Edward. 2012. 'Visible earshot': The returning voice of Susan Howe. *Cambridge Quarterly* 41 (4): 397–421. https://www.jstor.org/stable/i40138538.

Batchen, Geoffrey. 2006. In *Electricity made visible. In new media, old media: A history and theory reader*, ed. Wendy H.K. Chun and Thomas Keenan, 12–25. London: Routledge.

Blanchot, Maurice. 2010. *The space of literature*. Lincoln: University of Nebraska Press.

Bruns, Gerald. 2009. Voices of construction: on Susan Howe's poetry and poetics (a citational ghost story). *Contemporary Literature* 50 (1): 28–53. https://jstor.org/stable/20616412.

Cueff, Alain. 1999. The meantime of light. *James Welling: New Abstractions*, 9–12. Hanover: Sprengel Museum Hannover.

DuPlessis, Rachel Blau. 1990. *The pink guitar: Writing as feminist practice*. London: Routledge.

Dworkin, Craig. 1996. 'Waging political babble': Susan Howe's visual prosody and the politics of noise. *Word & Image* 12 (4): 389–405. https://doi.org/10.1080/02666286.1996.10435440.

———. 2003. *Reading the illegible*. Evanston: Northwestern University Press.

———. 2013. *No medium*. Cambridge: Massachusetts Institute of Technology Press.

Eco, Umberto. 1995. *The search for the perfect language*. Hoboken: Blackwell.

Elcott, Noam M. 2008. The shadow of the world: James Welling's cameraless and abstract photography. *Aperture* 190: 30–39. https://jstor.org/stable/i24473171.

Emerson, Ralph Waldo. 2004. *Emerson: Poems*. New York: Everyman's Library.

Emerson, Lori. 2008. My digital Dickinson. *The Emily Dickinson Journal* 17: 55–76. https://doi.org/10.1353/EDJ.0.0183.

Emerson, Ralph Waldo. 2012. *The annotated Emerson*. Ed. David Mikics. Cambridge: Belknap Press.

Fordyce, James. 1796. *Sermons to young women, in two volumes*. Boston: Millar and Cadell.

Gitelman, Lisa. 2008. *Always already new: Media, history, and the data of culture*. Cambridge: Massachusetts Institute of Technology Press.

Golding, Alan. 2002. 'Drawings with words': Susan Howe's visual poetics. In *We who love to be astonished: Experimental women's writing and performance poetics*, ed. Laura Hinton and Cynthia Hogue, 152–116. Tuscaloosa: University of Alabama Press.

Harkey, John. 2013. Lattice-glyphs: The intensive 'small poetry' of Susan Howe's recent work. *Arizona Quarterly: A Journal of American Literature, Culture, and Theory* 69 (4): 159–200. https://doi.org/10.1353/arq.2013.0027.
Harris, Kaplan Page. 2006. Susan Howe's art and poetry, 1968–1974. *Contemporary Literature* 47 (3): 440–471. https://doi.org/10.1353/cli.2007.0002.
Howe, Susan. 1989. The difficulties interview. *The Difficulties* 3 (2): 17–27.
———. 1990. *The Europe of trusts*. New York: New Directions.
———. 1993a. *The birth-mark: Unsettling the wilderness in American literary history*. Middletown: Wesleyan University Press.
———. 1993b. *The nonconformist's memorial*. New York: New Directions.
———. 1999. *Pierce-arrow*. New York: New Directions.
———. 2003. *The midnight*. New York: New Directions.
———. 2007a. *My Emily Dickinson*. New York: New Directions.
———. 2007b. *Souls of the Labadie tract*. New York: New Directions.
———. 2010a. Discussion during the Kelly Writer's House fellows program. Interview by Al Filreis. *PennSound*. https://media.sas.upenn.edu/pennsound/authors/Howe/03-23-10/Howe-Susan_Fellows-Discussion_KWH-UPenn_03-23-2010.mp3. Accessed 4 June 2014.
———. 2010b. *That this*. New York: New Directions.
———. 2012. The art of poetry no. 97. Interview by Maureen N. McLane. *The Paris Review* 203: 145–169.
———. 2013. *Sorting facts; or, nineteen ways of looking at marker*. New York: New Directions.
———. 2014. *Spontaneous particulars: The telepathy of archives*. New York: New Directions.
Howe, Susan, and James Welling. 2010. *Frolic architecture*. New York: Grenfell Press.
Hugnet, Georges. 1981. The dada spirit in painting. In *The dada painters and poets*, ed. Robert Motherwell, 123–196. Belknap: Cambridge.
Irigaray, Luce. 1985. *This sex which is not one*. Ithaca: Cornell University Press.
Janeck, Gerald. 1996. *Zaum: The transrational poetry of Russian futurism*. San Diego: San Diego State University Press.
Jennings, Chelsea. 2015. Susan Howe's facsimile aesthetic. *Contemporary Literature* 56 (4): 660–694. https://muse.jhu.edu/article/611150.
Laxton, Susan. 2012. White shadows: Photograms around 1922. In *Inventing abstraction: 1910–1925*, ed. Leah Dickerman, 332–335. New York: MoMA.
Michaels, Walter Benn. 2006. *The shape of the signifier: 1967 to the end of history*. Princeton: Princeton University Press.
Montgomery, Will. 2010. *The poetry of Susan Howe: History, theology, authority*. London: Palgrave.

OED (*Oxford English Dictionary*). n.d.. https://www.oed.com. Accessed 27 June 2017.

Palattella, John. 1995. An end of abstraction: An essay on Susan Howe's historicism. *Denver Quarterly* 29 (3): 74–97.

Reed, Brian. 2004. 'Eden or ebb of the sea': Susan Howe's word squares and postlinear poetics. *Postmodern Culture* 14 (2). https://pomoculture.org/2013/09/18/eden-or-ebb-of-the-sea-susan-howes-word-squares-and-postlinear-poetics. Accessed 4 June 2014.

Rotman, Brian. 2008. *Becoming beside ourselves: The alphabet, ghosts, and distributed human being*. Durham: Duke University Press.

Sedgwick, Eve Kosofsky. 2003. *Touching feeling*. Durham: Duke University Press.

Spieker, Sven. 2008. *The big archive*. Cambridge: Massachusetts Institute of Technology Press.

Stevens, Wallace. 1990. *The collected poems of Wallace Stevens*. New York: Knopf.

Stokes, Hugh. 1992. *French art in French life*. London: P. Allan.

Thoreau, Henry David. 1980. *A week on the Concord and Merrimack rivers*. Princeton: Princeton University Press.

Welling, James. 2004. James Welling. Interview by Deven Golden. *BOMB*. https://bombmagazine.org/articles/2004/04/01/james-welling. Accessed 4 June 2014.

———. 2008. Abstract, representational, and so forth. Interview by Chris Balaschak. *Surface* 4: 153–159.

CHAPTER 3

Deep Erasure in Yedda Morrison's Darkness

In this chapter, I consider the process of erasure as emergent poetic methodology: a tool for resisting anthropocentrism by disfiguring the medium to simulate a wilderness experience, producing in the reader a sense of radical self-negation and awareness of pluralities of agency both human and nonhuman.[1] To achieve such a wilderness experience, Yedda Morrison's *Darkness* performs what the author calls a "biocentric" erasure on Joseph Conrad's *Heart of Darkness*. By reworking *Heart of Darkness* from an ecological perspective, Morrison updates Conrad's canonical critique of British imperialism with an eye toward contemporary debates on carbon- and climate-imperialism.[2] Methodologically, according to Morrison, a biocentric reading involves whiting-out all references to humans in Conrad's text, while maintaining the original print orientation

---

[1] Max Oelschlaeger records the long tradition of turning to "wilderness," whether literal or figurative, for such philosophical musings. To be clear, Oelschlaeger and Morrison alike acknowledge that a purely natural wilderness does not exist, but both are invested in the power of the *idea* of wilderness. My reading of a wilderness experience as a media effect rather than a "natural" encounter is informed by Levi Bryant's essay on "Wilderness Ontology" (2011).

[2] Morrison's reference for this concept is likely Mike Davis's *Late Victorian Holocausts: El Niño Famines and the Making of the Third World* (2001), an analysis of the relationship between global economic forces and climate patterns in the late-nineteenth century. Morrison made reference to this text as a source of inspiration for *Darkness* in a reading in Buffalo, NY, on November 12, 2014.

© The Author(s), under exclusive license to Springer Nature Switzerland AG 2025
T. W. Matteson, *Emergent Poetics*, Modern and Contemporary Poetry and Poetics, https://doi.org/10.1007/978-3-031-70737-7_3

for the text that remains, leaving sparse arrangements of words ("river- / light") and even the occasional blank page. The wilderness philosopher Max Oelschlaeger writes, "Biocentrists take life rather than the human species as the central verity and thus assign value to all other things relative to life" (1991, p. 293). Yet I suggest that Morrison's view of biocentrism disrupts even the idea of a center. I read *Darkness* in relation to two different traditions: erasure poetics and Deep Ecology, an anthrodecentric environmental movement founded on the principle of the equal value of all life. I find a striking methodological incongruity between *Darkness* and the genre of erasure poetry, with which it is commonly associated. This chapter follows Morrison's lead in proposing an erasure *poetics* (a theory of poetry rather than a genre of poetry) inflected by Deep Ecology, a poetics which I intend to call "deep erasure." Deep erasure in the manner of *Darkness* recuperates a rarely discussed principle of Deep Ecology—biospherical egalitarianism—to advance an emergent poetics that refuses to participate in the hierarchy privileging human narratives over nonhuman ones. Rather, Morrison's *Darkness* affords us the opportunity to explore a nonhuman ethic in the practice of erasure in other poetic media, given that her project is explicitly directed toward "turning a story into a picture" (2014a).

3.1 Activating the Scenery

In the artist's statement on her work called *Darkness*—which exists in several different forms, from a gallery exhibit, to an e-book, to a mass market paperback—Yedda Morrison writes that "the project aims to activate the backdrop or scenery upon which this story of colonial horror unfolds, and in doing so attend to the latent narratives of any organic, non-human remains" (2014). Morrison's invocation of "latent narratives" deserves further explanation—if we read *Darkness* as Morrison's attempt to tune in to those narratives, that may put *Darkness* in conversation with Howe's project of attempting to "tenderly lift from the dark side of history, voices that are anonymous, slighted—inarticulate" (Howe 1990, p. 14). Additionally, a focus on "latent narratives" will allow us to read *Darkness* in context of a prominent trend in ecological thought—examining the role of language (or logocentrism, perhaps) as a causal factor in resourcism and exploitation of the natural world. Christopher Manes, for example, writes, "Nature *is* silent in our culture (and in literate societies generally) in the sense that the status of being a speaking subject is jealously guarded as an exclusively human prerogative" (1992, p. 339). Morrison responds to the condition of silence Manes identifies.

But what form do these so-called latent narratives take? In *Darkness*, Morrison takes Conrad's first paragraph of *Heart of Darkness*—"The *Nellie*, a cruising yawl, swung her anchor without a flutter of the sails, and was at rest. The flood had made, the wind was nearly calm, and being bound down the river, the only thing for it was to come to and wait for the turn of the tide"—and turns it into—"flood / wind / river, / tide" (2008, p. 3; 2012, p. 3). As this comparison reveals, *Darkness* does not feature what could be considered a conventional narrative, nothing resembling identifiable characters or a sequence of events, nor even conventional grammar. I would suggest that narrative, in the sense that Morrison invokes, is instead an attitude on the part of the reader rather than a formal quality inherent in the text: *Darkness* asks the reader to afford to its textual remnants the same esteem, even reverence, with which readers approach Conrad's characters.

The text itself signals this relationship to metaphor by maintaining the same formatting and layout of the original Signet Classics version of *Heart of Darkness*. On the cover, the Signet Classics logo has been blacked-out at the top, but in the center of the cover Joseph Conrad's name still looms, only partially whited-out, as if immersed in a dense fog: the tail of the "J" and the serifs of the "H" are visible, as are the top and bottom of the "C" and the curve of the "D." Morrison's name, in all lowercase, is superimposed over the "JOSEPH." "HEART" and "OF" are completely whited-out, but "DARKNESS" is totally unobscured, emerging from the black background in an eerie orange font. The visual appearance of the text resembles a photocopy, granting the book an evidentiary quality. Indeed, the grainy look of the facsimile pages, coupled with the partially legible text, recalls redacted government documents, though the excised text is whited- rather than blacked-out. This distinction makes the whiteout lines nearly, but not completely blend into the background white space of the page, almost as if, instead of concealing text, Morrison has attempted (and failed) to *unsay* much of Conrad's text.

The parasitic relationship between Morrison's *Darkness* and Conrad's *Heart of Darkness* constitutes a shift in subject from nineteenth-century European imperialism to twenty-first-century climate imperialism. Yet, the conventional force of this supposed critique is undercut by the fraught relationship between Conrad's text and the context of its initial publication. As Hunt Hawkins notes in "Conrad's Critique of Imperialism in *Heart of Darkness*," the evidence for a strong critique against imperialism in all its forms is complicated in Conrad's work by the narrative juxtaposition of Belgian colonialism (deemed "wasteful") and British ("efficient") colonialism (1979, p. 286). More recently, Matthew C. Connolly takes a periodical studies approach to Conrad's novel, reading it in context of its initial publication in *Blackwood's Edinburgh Magazine*. Connolly finds that the British nationalist rhetoric surrounding Conrad's text in *Blackwood's* shapes how we should understand *Heart of Darkness*'s relationship to imperialism: "the text's indictment of humanitarian atrocities was folded into an argument for British exceptionalism" (2016, p. 93). From this perspective, it would be facile to suppose that Morrison simply updates Conrad's "imperialist critique" to make a similar critique of the Global North's climate imperialism. In fact, there are more obvious parallels between Morrison's recognition of the way Conrad's text silences nature and Chinua Achebe's famous analysis of the way *Heart of Darkness* omits African voices (2016). Rather, by analyzing Morrison's method of "biocentric erasure," by interrogating each term individually, and by synthesizing these terms into a theory of medium, I hope to show how the possibilities of reading *Darkness* extend beyond critique, advancing instead an affirmative politics of wilderness.

The success of *Darkness*, however, is that Morrison's project is not purely negative. Indeed, though much of the conceptual weight comes from its relationship to the canonical status of Conrad's text, *Darkness* itself stands on its own as a poetic work. The experience of the reader is foregrounded here in the text, immersed as one becomes in the visual play of words down the (now predominantly white) page, and the atmosphere created by the imagistic nature of the text. The text yields a kind of tonal arc, moving from images of light and fecundity in the early chapters to apocalyptic visions of total darkness by the final page. Words like "luminous," "brilliance," and "radiance" open the first pages (2012, pp. 3, 4). But in the final pages, the reader is immersed in "darkness deepened," "dark—dark," until the final words of the text consume all: "immense darkness" (2012, pp. 128, 131, 132). Beyond the mood that the shift from light to dark produces, the interplay between light and dark in the text may also be read reflexively, in the contrast between black type and a white page. In fact, typographically and thematically, light and darkness evoke two contradictory senses: on a basic typographic level, the white space on the page is "light" and the ink of the text is "dark." Yet the movement from light to darkness through the text also tracks with the movement from legibility and conventional narrative—the ability to "see through" Conrad's novel as a window—toward the darkness of Morrison's text—both in its grammatical opacity and its emphasis on the visible surface of the page, which acts as a barrier to conventional interpretation. The term "river" appears several times throughout the *Darkness* as well, evoking both the image of a natural river and the typographic "rivers" (the coincidence of blank spaces between words that seem to run down a typed page) that have overflown their banks thanks to Morrison's erasures. Perhaps it is no coincidence that the first word in the text is "flood": by widening the typographic rivers in *Heart of Darkness*, Morrison has unleashed a regenerative, bewildering flood.

Indeed, Morrison's *Darkness* offers the reader an overwhelming experience, offering no easy passage through the text. This condition of bewilderment, a recognition that conventional reading practices offer limited utility here, is mirrored in the text: by my count, the word "wilderness" appears seventeen times throughout the work, usually in isolation, but occasionally as part of a phrase retained from Conrad's original text, as in "wilderness stink" and "wilderness burst" (2012, pp. 57, 82). The usage of the word "wilderness" parallels the tonal shift from light to dark in the text since it appears more frequently in the second half of the text, a full six appearances of the word coming in the final thirty pages. This reading makes clear that, as I indicated above, the "narrative" of Morrison's text is an attitude on the part of the reader, in fact, a participatory narrative in which the reader's increasing bewilderment within the text parallels the increasing awareness of the biocentrism of the text. Though the reader is often "at a loss," it is precisely this experience that affords *Darkness* its essential force.

Early in Morrison's poetic career, in the pages of *Tripwire*, a journal she founded and co-edited with poet David Buuck, she writes, "do we enter the unknown to seek solely that which is recognizable? in this the poem short-circuits. if we fully recognized the limits of our time on the planet it would be incapacitating or incendiary" (1998, p. 43). In this passage, Morrison seems to reject a poetry that is simply an indirect expression of events or emotions, but instead pays attention to the poem's context, its status as an object in the world. Already, in this piece, entitled, "integrity, my new fragrance," Morrison is working out the sense of scale that undergirds *Darkness*: that perhaps the human subject is not the telos of the natural world, a sense of scale inhibited by anthropocentrism that can only be experienced through an encounter with the wilderness—that which exceeds human interpretation for the purposes of emergent poetics: to forestall interpretation and, ultimately, instrumentalization and exploitation. This short essay illustrates Morrison's own poetics in the form of a critique of the aesthetic standards that are prevalent even among nontraditional or experimental poetries. With *Darkness*, Morrison does "enter the unknown," not to conquer, as Conrad's characters do, or to "seek only the recognizable," but to listen, to render visible/audible a voice that never ceases to speak, a voice that we cannot identify as our own, but as Other: *vox naturae*.

For Morrison, however, our ability to tune in to the voice of nature, to participate in its "latent narratives," is limited by the incommensurability between human language and the natural world. Of this last point, Morrison is (rightly, as a century of Saussurian linguistics would suggest) highly skeptical, leaving us, as she does, in "immense darkness." In the statement on *Darkness*, Morrison writes,

> Of course language is too blunt an instrument, our conflations of economy and tongue too deeply entrenched to all for a clean excision. All language is political, each extraction economic, every vowel a hybrid of nature and technology, my erasures tentative and flawed. The project's failure to fulfill its promise of an articulated, pre-human wilderness is precisely its point; there is no other, and no Eden without Eve, only an endlessly precarious entanglement. (2014)

Our endeavor then, must be to both trace the contours and qualities of the wilderness Morrison plucks out of *Heart of Darkness* and to interrogate the reasons for *Darkness*'s failure (some of which Morrison lists above). Is the failure in the articulation? Is language too fraught with politics to convey the voice of nature? Or perhaps, as Gertrude Stein writes, "there is no there there." That is, perhaps it stands to reason that not only can we not express nature absent humanity, but we cannot even perceive it: to observe it would be to change it. The latter is more likely, given Morrison's invocation of "entanglement" at the conclusion of the passage. "Entanglement," so often preceded by "quantum," refers to the way in which we (typically physicists) cannot observe a system without being implicated in said system, and thereby changing it.[3] And indeed, *Darkness* bears this out, by demonstrating that humanity cannot be removed (nor should it be). Biocentrism as Morrison conceives of it is not anti-human but merely a recognition that if the human voices are not erased, no other "voices" can be heard.

Yet as I hope to suggest, Morrison herself offers too limited a reading of her own work, foreclosing on the potential of *Darkness* to promote a wilderness experience, however tenuous. Morrison is certainly correct that language is blunt—political, entrenched, and so on. I am more interested, though, in the methodological implications of *Darkness*, rather than their products (the resulting text), and so wish to defer the question of the failure of *Darkness* to "represent" nature. Instead, I hope to explore the ways in which the methodology of erasure produces a *simulation* of a wilderness experience. In this, *Darkness* does not fail; indeed, as Morrison herself notes in "integrity, my bold new fragrance," "while there is inside there is no outside" (1998, p. 45). *Darkness* is unable to represent an "articulated, pre-human wilderness" precisely because to such a wilderness does not exist. Poetic erasure acknowledges this impossibility while still holding on to the potentiality that such an intervention in a textual, mediated environment can result in insight into the relations between and among humans and nonhumans in an ecosystem.

To understand *Darkness*, as I have suggested, we must first understand its methods. The first printed edition of Morrison's work was published as *Darkness (Chapter 1)* by Little Red Leaves, an online poetry journal that also publishes electronic and print-on-demand versions of poetry books and chapbooks. The text itself, a facsimile of Morrison's erasure of Chap. 1 of *Heart of Darkness* comprises the bulk of the edition, but the first thing we see is not text but image: William Notman's photograph "Around the Campfire, Caribou Hunting Series." This photograph, from 1866, features four men sitting around a campfire, in front of what appears to be a rudimentary hunting tent or shelter. The men are illuminated by the light of the campfire, as coniferous trees fade into shadow in the background. Below this, Morrison has included her treatment of Notman's image commissioned by the McCord Museum of Canadian History. The men are gone, as is their fire and their shelter. All that remains are trees and mist. The caption reads, "Pre-Colonial Forest in Fog (a Biocentric

---

[3] For an extended discussion on entanglement and the observer effect, see *Meeting the Universe Halfway*, by Karen Barad (2007).

reading of William Notman's 'Around the Campfire, Caribou Hunting Series')." We immediately understand why Morrison includes these images in this edition of *Darkness*: the text and the images have been produced by the same method: a biocentric erasure.

As the photographic erasures demonstrate, Morrison again leverages biocentrism into an erasure of the human—the inclusion of these images in this first edition of *Darkness* suggest that they serve to illustrate both the text and the method by which the text was produced. Consider the language with which Morrison introduces each piece. On the title page of the Little Red Leaves edition of *Darkness*, Morrison has inscribed "re-animating the pre-colonial wilderness: a biocentric reading of Joseph Conrad's Heart of Darkness" (2009). Similarly, at the conclusion of the text, Morrison writes of both *Darkness* and the photograph, "This work imagines a wood/world prior to, and free from, imperial intervention" (2009). There is a circular quality to Morrison's description of her method, a subtle density to the idea of "re-animating the pre-colonial." Is this what follows post-colonialism? A re-animation? Is this a "wood/world" once alive but now requires resuscitation? Morrison's commentary on the "failure" of *Darkness* suggests the latter. Yet, the juxtaposition of the Notman image with the text of *Darkness* raises the stakes of the project far beyond the success or failure of an "authentic" expression of primordial nature. What is truly at stake is an emergent poetics, facilitated by an intervention in the print medium, that refuses the nature–culture binary—indeed, that refuses all hierarchies with respect to living things.

Complicating our reading of *Darkness* is the project's existence in multiple versions. As noted above, book versions were printed by Little Red Leaves (*Darkness Chapter 1*) and by Make Now Press. Additionally, Morrison exhibited enlarged pages from *Darkness* in Republic Gallery in Vancouver, which she describes in the artist's statement on her website, and staged an interactive installation at LACE (Los Angeles Contemporary Exhibitions), in which gallery attendees were invited to perform their own version of a biocentric erasure on large-scale reproductions of *Heart of Darkness*. The instability of *Darkness* as a "finished" work only adds to its potential as a wilderness text—its multiplicity of forms exceeds easy definition and categorization and resists the hierarchical impulse to identify an authoritative version of the text (and, consequently, a definitive reading of the text).[4]

---

[4] See Marjorie Perloff, *Differentials: Poetry, Poetics, Pedagogy*, on "'differential poetry,' that is, poetry that does not exist in a single material state but can vary according to the medium of presentation: printed book, cyberspace, installation, or oral rendition" (2004, p. 173).

3.2 Genre Trouble

To fully appreciate the political implications of *Darkness*, we must first consider this work in its most commonly cited context: the tradition erasure poetry.[5] Under whatever banner—erasure, deletionism, removal, palimpsest, absence, silence, corrosion, abstraction, redaction, transparency, aeration, perforation—poetry created by means of erasure has a contentious history. Indeed, erasure poetry does not seem to cohere in a single tradition, but rather, as scholars tend to point out, breaks down along methodological or thematic lines: "erasure poetry" is often characterized as poetry *about* erasure or absence (McHale's (2005) "Poetry Under Erasure," for example), as much as poetry produced *by* erasure.[6] And if the mere definition of the genre of erasure poetry remains the subject of debate—"what counts as erasure poetry?"—the significance of the genre's political project is even more difficult to agree upon. Yet, *Darkness* is often cited as a prime example of erasure poetry, so it becomes necessary to further define the genre in context of which *Darkness* is currently being read.

In his essay, "A Brief History of Erasure Poetics," Travis MacDonald traces erasure poetry back to what he calls the "accidental" erasures in the fragments of Sappho (a questionable designation), but quickly moves to the mid-twentieth century and the Oulipo, whose experiments in the poetry of constraint by way of lipogram—omitting one or more letters in a given text—MacDonald characterizes as the forerunners of what we now think of as erasure poetry (2009, par. 29). MacDonald, for his part, is focused particularly on methodological, rather than thematic, erasure. The works he discusses were produced by erasing, obscuring, or otherwise abstracting text from a found document. The two key examples MacDonald offers are Ronald Johnson's *Radi os* (1977) and Tom Phillips' *A Humument: A Treated Victorian Novel* (1970). While Johnson's text literally erases much of Milton's *Paradise Lost*, leaving a new, shorter poem in its place, Phillips' work paints over sections of text from Mallock's 1892 novel *A Human Document*. MacDonald carefully parses these two examples, noting, "Johnson's work was based on and inspired largely by musical theory, while Phillips claims to have taken his initial cues from the 'cut-up' techniques of Williams Burroughs" (2009, par. 70). More

---

[5] See Ron Silliman's "Poetry Written With an Eraser" (2010) for example.
[6] McHale's (2005) text is about poetry whose subject, rather than method of composition, is erasure.

crucial, perhaps, than the inspiration for these projects is their actual methodology. MacDonald notes, "Where Johnson's adaptation was concerned primarily with the calculated *removal* of the host text, Phillips focuses his creative attention on the *covering up* or *masking* of Mallock's original work" (2009, par. 73). Johnson's text is mostly white space, with the words he did allow to remain scattered around the page in their original orientation, but Phillips's work covers the much of original text with drawings and designs. Interestingly, Morrison's *Darkness* seems to synthesize the methods of these two texts: the finished work looks a bit more like *Radi os*, and yet, since it is presented in facsimile instead of being re-typeset, *Darkness* also gives the impression that the whiteout has covered or masked Conrad's original text in the manner of *A Humument* (though *Darkness* substitutes Phillips' drawings and designs with white space).

MacDonald's perspective on the history of erasure sits firmly within the mainstream of scholarly discourse the genre of erasure poetry. Whether in depth or in passing, most of the literature on erasure poetry cites either *Radi os* or *A Humument*, or both. Yet, what is problematic is the cultural significance MacDonald and others ascribe to erasure poetry as a genre. What follows is MacDonald's argument about what is at stake in erasure poetry, what he calls its "common intent": "to fully enact and embody the naturally evolving processes of erasure in their work and to thereby assist in the reclamation of our language and culture one text at a time" (2009, par. 7). The plural possessive is antithetical to erasure poetry in the manner of *Darkness*, so we either need to identify a new tradition in context of which to read *Darkness*, or we need to construct new ways of reading the current tradition of erasure poetry. MacDonald's further clarification of the problem which this supposed reclamation purports to solve does nothing to contradict these suspicions. He writes, "It seems that the written word lost some of its divine luster over the last half century because of overuse, if not outright abuse. Paperback novels, magazines, newspapers, junk mail and now the internet have all contributed to the cultural decay of the textual object" (2009, par. 38). MacDonald holds up works of erasure poetry as a kind of canonical vandalism, and at the same time seems to lament the disruption of the canon's hold on cultural standards, while also indicating that erasure poetry can participate in a kind of renewal of the aura of the textual object (2009, par. 39). This, I suggest, is the essence of "shallow erasure."

In "The Near Transitive Properties of the Political and Poetical: Erasure," Solmaz Sharif offers a more fully formed appraisal of erasure as a poetic method. Equating erasure with the U.S. government's practices of redaction (erasure of text) and rendition (erasure of bodies) during the wars in Afghanistan and Iraq, Sharif writes, "The first time I confronted erasure as an aesthetic tactic I was horrified. I don't remember exactly when or what it was … I know I thought of erasure as what a state does" (2013). In contrast with MacDonald's view of erasure poetry, the genre, Sharif is much more ambivalent about erasure, the method: "the proliferation of erasure as a poetic tactic in the United States is happening alongside a proliferation of our awareness of it as a state tactic. And, it seems, many erasure projects today hold these things as unrelated." Sharif recognizes the power of erasure as a state tactic, and the potential of poetic erasure as a method to subvert this state tactic, proposing alternative objectives of poetic erasure that have nothing to do with "the reclamation of our language and culture." She suggests:

1. Highlight via illegibility and silence an original erasure (e.g. Jen Bervin's Dickinson Fascicles or Phil Metres' Abu Ghraib Arias)
2. Collapse time and instance between dead and living (e.g. "The dead do not cease in the grave." Srikanth Reddy, Voyager, p. 3)
3. Expose author's authority and, therefore, role as culpable participant (e.g. "the very fact of mutilating the text broke the spell the complete text has on us. I use the word 'mutilate' with great deliberation here since I was deeply aware at the time I worked on Zong! that the intent of the transatlantic slave trade was to mutilate—languages, cultures, people, communities and histories—in the effort of a great capitalist enterprise. And I would argue that erasure is intrinsic to colonial and imperial forces. It's an erasure that continues up to the present." M. NourbeSe Philip)
4. Care for what is left behind so that erasure has an additive or highlighting effect (e.g. "my first encounter with the text as a potential palimpsest for erasure was reading the words "If it had no pencil, / Would it try mine – li—the first words attributed to Dickinson in 1861. I took a pencil and circled those words. In the next three poems I circled phrases: "a Flag"—"Victory"—"Martyrs"—"Streaks of Meteor – / Upon a Planet's Blind" and realized that I could work with these beginning poems as erasures." Janet Holmes)

5. Render incomplete a text to invite collaboration between reader and text (e.g. while not an intended erasure, If Not Winter, Sappho's fragments, Anne Carson trans.)
6. Point to the nearly infinite possibilities and infinite centers of a single text (e.g. any appropriation). (2003)

In context of Sharif's alternative objectives, Morrison's method of biocentric erasure that results in the text of *Darkness* might be read as an attempt to (in Sharif's words) "Care for what is left behind so that erasure has an additive or highlighting effect." Care, that is, for the language left behind after the excision of the human, and, by extension, the "voice" of nature.

The lesson of Sharif's approach is that poetic erasure—the method, the source text, the results—exists in and as a medium within a social, historical, and cultural context. Attention to this medium supplants the genre question with a far richer set of inquiries. This, if nothing else, is the lesson of *Darkness*: its contribution to the methodology is one of "deep erasure." In its attempt to envisage and perform biocentrism, *Darkness* explicitly suppresses, rather than reclaims, the anthropocentric categories of "our language and culture," foregrounding and disrupting the medium of the source text. By suppressing anthropocentrism, *Darkness* demonstrates just how dubious such a project as linguistic and cultural reclamation is. Instead, *Darkness* interrogates the possibility of what Max Oelschlaeger might call an ecological reconciliation—an attempt to undo the violence of anthropocentric erasure perpetrated by conventional human narratives (1991, pp. 271–272).[7] By removing references to humanity from *Heart of Darkness*, Morrison resists precisely the kind of anthropocentrism that MacDonald suggests is the "common intent" of erasure poetry. In its place, we find a kind of biocentric "flatness of information" that Cooney critiques, in the form of an attention to the "latent narratives" of the wilderness. That is, if information is flattened, then narratives of human endeavors do not exceed nonhuman narratives in terms of value. Crucially, reading Morrison's work in context of the history and critical reception of erasure poetry demonstrates not only that the stakes of the erasure methodology of *Darkness* are much higher than most scholars have recognized but that these scholarly treatments of erasure-based works in general tend

---

[7] Just as Susan Howe resists the term "recovery" to describe her archival works: "I don't want to be so arrogant as to say these are recoveries. Maybe certain people find me" (2012, p. 146). Recovery, like reclamation, implies possession.

to foreclose upon, rather than advance, the political potential of erasure poetics.

What if we read *Darkness* through MacDonald's framework? If for example, we pointed out that Morrison's erasure does, in fact, attempts to reclaim language from its overdetermination by imperialist politics? While this may be true, it fails to exhaust the full potential of *Darkness*. For if we insist on reducing Morrison's project to a drama of anthropocentric action, we run contrary to the very intent of Morrison's erasure: to foreground the latent narratives of the wilderness. If all that is at stake in *Darkness* is a critique of Conrad's literary imperialism (or his failed critique of European imperialism), the consequence is that wilderness—the evasive object of Morrison's project, is again relegated to the background, the scenery. There can be no "precarious entanglement" if there is nothing substantial with which the human actors can be entangled. Erasure poetics, from this view, must constitute a rich field of possibilities in which each gesture, each scrub of the eraser, each brush of liquid paper, each press of the delete key opens the work to ecological reconciliation by creating space where nonhuman entities—medialogical, biological, abiological—can enter the text on their own terms, rather than as metaphors for human experience.

3.3 Man / The Chosen

Morrison's reconfiguration of the stakes of erasure poetics comes into sharper relief when we read *Darkness* alongside its most obvious precedent: Ronald Johnson's *Radi os*. As Ron Silliman notes in a podcast entitled "Poetry Written with an Eraser," these two works bear some similarities. Both are erasures of canonical texts, and pre-erasure setting of *Darkness* is a nameless pre-colonial wilderness while the pre-erasure setting of *Radi os* is its archetype—the Garden of Eden. Both Johnson's and Morrison's texts meddle with the original authors' portrayal of the natural world as pure wilderness ready to be civilized. Additionally, Johnson anticipates Morrison's project of "turning a story into a picture," writing in the preface to *Radi os* that "Each page … is a single picture" (2005, p. ix). Both Johnson and Morrison explore the possibilities of re-mediating a textual object into a visual one. But on the very first page of *Radi os*, the similarities break down, their projects diverging, as Johnson writes (or excavates),

>   O   tree
>   into the World,
>   Man
>
>   the chosen
>   Rose out of Chaos:
>
>   song, (2005, p. 3)

Whatever his politics, whatever his methods, Johnson's invocation of "Man / the chosen" here runs at cross purposes with Morrison's methodological commitment to biocentric erasure, since the central thrust of this page announces an unabashed and even triumphal anthropocentrism, perhaps even more than Milton's original text. Additionally, *Radi os*, despite its emergence from within Milton's text, is "original" in the sense that Johnson himself selected which words to erase and which to retain, whereas Morrison's *Darkness* was composed by way of (admittedly subjective) constraint—*biocentric* erasure. But *Radi os* cannot be so easily dismissed—its project is too valuable and its position in the tradition of erasure poetry too established to overlook. Additionally, *Radi os* is a clear antecedent of *Darkness*, given visual appearance, canonical source text, and theme, regardless of its divergence in methodology, and an extended reading of *Radi os* will serve to further illustrate the contours of deep erasure.

If *Radi os* is not a biocentric erasure (and it certainly is not, by Morrison's definition), what manner of erasure is it, and how should we describe its methods? Its most fervid celebration comes in the form of Guy Davenport's afterword to the Flood Editions publication of the poem. Davenport, in a passage that also appears on the rear cover of the Flood printing, writes,

> *Radi os* is a meditation, first of all, on grace. It finds in Milton's poems those clusters of words which were originally a molecular intuition of the complex harmony of nature whereby eyesight loops back to its source in the sun, the earth, the tree, our cousin animals, the spiralling [*sic*] galaxies, and mysteriously to the inhuman black of empty space. (2005, p. 104)

From this description of the *Radi os*, though its methods might differ, its message seems strikingly like that of *Darkness*, particularly in Davenport's invocation of "the complex harmony of nature," which is perhaps a more optimistic version of Morrison's concept of an "endlessly precarious entanglement."

Harmony is certainly an appropriate metaphor for Johnson's work, which as the author's preface indicates, is inspired both by music and by visual art. Johnson describes hearing a recording of Lukas Foss's "Baroque Variations," in which the conductor inserts moments of inaudibility and improvisation into Handel's Concerto Grosso Op. 6. No. 12, of which Foss says, "The inaudible moments leave holes in Handel's music (I composed the holes)" (2005, p. ix).[8] Johnson, like Foss, is a composer of holes, though his text is more perforated than "Baroque Variations." Rather than a true adaptation of *Paradise Lost*, *Radi os* takes Milton's work as its lexicon, or, since Johnson maintains the original page alignment of the words, we might call *Paradise Lost* its "lexicontext." *Radi os* is written with Milton's words and emerges from within Milton's text. After hearing the Foss recording, Johnson says, he bought a copy of the 1892 edition of *Paradise Lost* and created a new poem by striking out parts of Milton's text. Unlike *Darkness*, which reproduces the treated text in facsimile, the most recent edition of *Radi os*, the Flood Editions printing of 2005, is not a facsimile of Johnson's original vandalism. Rather, the text has been typeset, maintaining as nearly as possible the spatial arrangement of words on the page from Milton's original text. Since Johnson retains the position of the words from Milton's poem, each page in *Radi os* features a scattering of words down the page, prompting Selinger to note "a certain purely visual, concrete element" (1992, p. 48).

Selinger's invocation of pure visuality gestures to another of Johnson's precedents (and fellow *Paradise Lost* vandal), William Blake, whose etchings serve as Johnson's methodological model, according to the preface to *Radi os*. McCaffery reads *Radi os* through the logic of Blakean etching, pointing out that "[r]ather than cutting away, relief etching involves a physical removal by means of corrosion" (2012, p. 31). *Radi os*, then, becomes a signature text in the tradition of what McCaffery calls "corrosive poetics," a compositional method that mirrors the effects of chemical corrosion. Concerning the resulting text, McCaffery writes, "By way of retinal tracking and excavation of a latent other poem, *Radi os* 'quotes' the inaudible Milton, a Milton that is not Milton's, thereby bringing to textual apposition Rimbaud's famous claim that 'I is another' linguistically reformulated as 'this text also holds an Other'" (2012, p. 33). Regarding

---

[8] My copy of the LP of *Baroque Variations* (performed by the Buffalo Philharmonic Orchestra and conducted by Foss, himself) also includes John Cage's *Concerto for Prepared Piano & Orchestra* performed by Yuji Takahashi.

retinal tracking, Johnson writes, or rather, sets in relief, "Seized / with eyes / under the flow" (2005, p. 80). This invocation of Rimbaud echoes Yedda Morrison's reference to the latent narratives that emerge from *Heart of Darkness* when, by way of erasure, the human narrative has been suppressed. McCaffery makes clear that corrosion is not a mere metaphor for Johnson's method but rather a transposition: "*Radi os* then is the product of a corrosive poetics, a relief composition received by Johnson as Blake's gift to him that transposes Blake's graphic method into typographic textuality, burning away large areas of the surface text with the aqua fortis of Johnson's own imagination" (2012, p. 31).[9]

We should not be so quick as to dismiss "imagination" as a non-physical and, consequently, a simplistically metaphorical application of the abundantly physical process of corrosion. Indeed, McCaffery argues that,

> In *The Marriage of Heaven and Hell*, relief etching emerges as a ready symbol for dispelling the Cartesian illusion of a mind-body dualism. As Blake writes, "the notion that man has a body distinct from his soul, is to be expunged; this I shall do by printing in the infernal method, by corrosives, which in Hell are salutary and medicinal, melting apparent surfaces away, and displaying the infinite that was hid." (2012, p. 31)

The mind, like the nitric acid in Blake's original method, is physically consequential; the mind, a physical phenomenon itself, possesses the ability to direct or suppress the senses, to either look at or look through "apparent surfaces." In the graphic medium, Blake's etchings, nitric acid serves as the corrosive agent, but, according to McCaffery's analysis of Johnson's transposition of "the infernal method" into the typographic medium, the mind itself stands in as the corrosive agent, hence "the aqua fortis of ... imagination."

Radi os, however, reverses the logic of Blake's "infernal method": rather than stripping the surface away to reveal the infinite, Johnson excises the infinite to draw greater attention to the apparent surfaces. As Erik Anderson argues, the predominant target of Johnson's removal is the spiritual and the divine—in other words, the infinite: "For Johnson, the mind was and is born of light—i.e., energy—not God as known to Milton" (2006, p. 5). Johnson's text corrodes away Milton's references to God; the resulting text meditates on the relationship of human intellection (the

---

[9] Just as Howe transposes the methodology of the photogram in her poetics.

physiological phenomenon) and the material universe. At one, point, *Radi os* presents us with these lines: "Man: him, through / Father / matter," evoking the kind of cognitive materialism which Anderson finds in Johnson's work\=. Anderson also writes, "*Radi os* makes the point that, if the act of reading is an act of seeing (or re-vision), then the act of seeing is an act of reading, whereby one reads the world and one's place in it" (2006, p. 4). *Radi os*, then, is a kind of astrological star map, distilling legible, largely anthropocentric constellations from Milton's night sky. Where an astrologer might find geometric shapes, animals, or human forms in the constellations, the consistent preoccupation of *Radi os* seems to be the human mind.

Indeed, though Guy Davenport identifies a complex harmony at work between humanity and nature in *Radi os*, the prevailing impression is one of anthropocentrism: "Man" is "the Chosen," and it is through the human senses that Johnson's poem meditates on the relationship between Man and Universe, with constant references to eyes and ears, vision and hearing. For Johnson (and, perhaps, for Blake), this kind of anthropocentrism may have been a ready alternative to the apparently spiritual/immaterial deity-centric world of Milton's *Paradise Lost*. But in retrospect, seen from the vantage point of Morrison's *Darkness*, Johnson's excision of the spiritual, which by process of elimination foregrounds the material and human, may have produced the opposite of its intended effect. If the "goal" of *Radi os* is indeed the awareness of the "complex harmony of nature," as Davenport suggests, then perhaps Johnson's anthropocentrism is like Milton's deity-centrism. Johnson supplants Milton's God—who in some interpretations of the Genesis story granted humanity dominion over nature—with the human mind, which still claims primacy (intellectual dominion?) over the natural world. Consider the following page from BOOK III of *Paradise Lost*, re-envisioned as O III from *Radi os*:

> Worlds,
> That both in him and all things,
>   drive
> deepest
>   Sun,
>   are all his works,
> created mind
>   Infinitude confined;
>   quintessence
>   turned to star (2005, p. 64)

Though Johnson's preface to the work makes clear that each page may be read as a single image in isolation, the previous page suggests that the subject of the above passage is "Man ... Alone" (2005, p. 63). The above passage implies that "Infinitude" has been confined within "mind"; the phrase "created mind" may be interpreted as "created [by means of] mind." This mind, or consciousness itself, in Johnson's work, is imbued with the creative energy that participated in the formation of the universe.

In this reading, we might further refine our understanding of Johnson's anthropocentrism as a more refined "cerebrocentrism," in which human consciousness is the evolutionary destiny of the universe. Of *ARK*, a project of more epic proportions than *Radi os*, Johnson writes that it is "Based on trinities, its cornerstones the eye, the ear, the mind" (2014, p. 312). In an interview from 1997, Johnson says, "I don't believe necessarily in God; I believe in a transcendence or something. I believe that brains were made to communicate with the universe. Life was always tending towards the human brain, so that the universe could start talking to itself" (p. 32). The human brain, for Johnson, is the telos of biology: mind is matter in its highest form. As we have seen above, such a sentiment is reflected in the text of *Radi os* itself. This is not at all unorthodox in the realm of erasure poetics. In his essay on *Radi os*, McCaffery directs us to Emmanuel Levinas, who argues that thought "is originally word-erasing—that is to say, symbolic. And because thought is symbolic, ideas can hook up with one another and create a connecting network ... [which] owes its value not so much to the fact that it connects one thought to another but rather to the fact that it guarantees the presence of one given thought *within* another" (quoted in McCaffery 2012, p. 30). Poetic erasure, from this perspective, is a kind of thought-simulation, in which the resulting spatiality becomes symbolic, the text that remains raising one thought from another, born like Athena from Zeus's brain.

But by evoking the symbolic, by simulating thought, this "word-erasing" often becomes "world-erasing."[10] This is precisely the situation to which Morrison's conception of biocentric erasure responds. By performing her biocentric erasure of an imperialist text, Morrison is both producing an erasure of human action and *correcting* an erasure of the

---

[10] This may be true of not only *Radi os* but of Conceptual Writing more broadly, but that line of argumentation is beyond the scope of this chapter.

natural world as perpetrated by human action. That is, Conrad's (and, it seems, his characters') instrumentalization of the continent of Africa as either an inanimate obstacle, a valuable resource, or a virgin land ready for conquering, effectively erases the continent itself, supplanted by the projection of man's own desires. A biocentric erasure, then, endeavors to de-instrumentalize the natural world by enacting an egalitarian valuation of all life, its biocentric constraint serving to actualize what Morrison has called "latent narratives" in the text. By contrast, we might read Johnson's poem, rich as it is with methodological implications, as cerebrocentric, essentially a reinscription of the Great Chain of Being, merely substituting human consciousness for God and assigning value to the rest of the universe of "beings" according to their availability to human perceptual faculties. But as we have seen in the previous chapter, anthropocentric interpretation may be suppressed to foreground unorthodox or otherwise marginalized details and voices. Morrison extends this logic with her concept of biocentric erasure—while we may begin to *read* in a way that attempts to neutralize the boundary between sense and nonsense, we may also begin to *compose* in a way that neutralizes the text's ontological hierarchy.

3.4 Metaphors on *Darkness*

While *Radi os* is indeed the most commonly cited precedent for Morrison's erasure—in source text, theme, and appearance—it differs greatly in methodology. To identify a true precedent for the method of biocentric erasure that Morrison has used to produce *Darkness*, I now turn to one of Johnson's contemporaries, Stan Brakhage, and his work in another medium: film. The turn to a visual medium such as film is, in fact, perfectly natural, given Morrison's description of her project as "turning a story into a picture." I argue that Brakhage's short film *Mothlight* represents precisely the kind of biocentric erasure that we find in Morrison's work. *Mothlight*, which Brakhage completed in 1963, more than a decade prior to Johnson's *Radi os*, is an example of what is commonly known as cameraless film—that is, a film produced without the use of a camera. As Fred Camper explains in the liner notes to the Criterion Collection edition of Brakhage's work, *Mothlight* was composed by collaging various materials—grass, leaves, moth wings—onto transparent tape corresponding to the size of 16 mm film stock. I turn to this film because, as we shall see, it bears striking resemblance to both the method of biocentric erasure and the wilderness politics of Morrison's *Darkness*.

Brakhage tells two different stories about the genesis of *Mothlight*. In the first, found in *Metaphors on Vision*, Brakhage is amid a filmmaker's version of writer's block when a moth in his workroom distracts him and enables him to continue working. In the second, from a later recorded interview, Brakhage claims that he had been watching moths fly toward electric light and get burned up, and he saw it as a metaphor for his quixotic pursuit of film art (*Mothlight*). It is not clear why this story changed over the years. The later version, though, does have a certain figurative richness to it that suggests embellishment or retroactive editing—perhaps a post-production memory. In any version, Brakhage begins pasting moth wings and other materials onto clear tape and *Mothlight* is born.

In 1997, Brakhage sat for an interview with Ronald Johnson and Jim Shedden as part of Shedden's documentary *Brakhage* (1998). This would not have been the first contact between Brakhage and Johnson—both were in San Francisco in the 1960s, and both associated with Robert Duncan. Later, Brakhage regularly cited Johnson's poetry as evidence of a kindred spirit. By way of illustrating his approach to film, Brakhage says,

> There are some who would caution us about our use of language, who would say that there's no point in saying things like 'primordial,' that it's ridiculous to talk about a camera that's invented in the late nineteenth century and a projection mode and so on, and then to talk about how its touching the primordial mind—they'd tell us it's absurd ... And I could make the case that film—just by the very fact that it was invented within the last century, or just a century ago—is beginning at a beginning, is fit to begin where anything began. And its closest kinship is cave painting. It's at a cave painting stage at best in its development. (2001, p. 31)

Brakhage's invocation of the primordial returns us to Morrison's uninhabited *Darkness*, but it also corresponds, more immediately, with Johnson's description of his long poem, *ARK* as "an Ivesian symphony," saying, "[Ives] was like me—he knew a lot about music, but he wanted to appear a *naïve*, to get back to where you don't know anything about art. And then you construct something. I was trying to forget about music and then start all over again" (2014, p. 579, italics in original). Brakhage, like Johnson, is preoccupied with a kind of back-to-basics foundationalism, his films often weaving together a kind of Modernist preoccupation with medium specificity with the anti-cultural values of the *Art Brut* movement. The motivating factor in Brakhage's primordial tendencies, as P. Adam Sitney points out, is Brakhage's theory of language: its tendency to distort—or rather, overdetermine—visual perception. For Brakhage, the common usage of language is what perpetuates the illusory divide between nature and culture. In the *Brakhage* interview, the filmmaker insists, "Except for poets, I think language is a damnation of human sensibility and in the blind mouths of politicians is destroying us all" (2001, p. 32). Brakhage objects to a model of vision that is all too contingent upon its ability to be easily assimilated into linguistic/rational frameworks. But Brakhage's clearest statement on his resistance to the linguistic "damnation of human sensibility" comes in his writing in his 1963 *Metaphors on Vision*. This, though Brakhage's first book, already formulates a sophisticated critique of logocentrism and advocates—unsurprisingly, from a filmmaker—a mind guided by vision that might serve to resist the language-mind.

In *Metaphors on Vision*, Brakhage begins, "Imagine an eye unruled by man-made laws of perspective, an eye unprejudiced by compositional logic, an eye which does not respond to the name of everything, but which must know each object in life through an adventure of perception" (1963, p. 1). Logic—that is, language—imposes a limitation on the fullness of perception. Brakhage asks, "How many colors are there in a field of grass to the crawling baby unaware of 'Green'?" (1963, p. 120). In his films, Brakhage is intent upon opening this field—to borrow his friend Robert Duncan's phrase—in both a literal and figurative sense. Brakhage's films work to restore a spectrum of vision obscured by language's limited taxonomy—as Morrison says, "language is too blunt an instrument." We may conceive of Brakhage's visual project, then, as a way of resisting the anthropocentric mode of seeing in which the natural world is merely a vacant mirror reflecting images of humanity back to itself. This manifests in Brakhage films through (often) the absence of narrative and perspective that is altogether unrecognizable as human: Deleuze cites Brakhage in *Cinema I: The Movement-Image*, as a filmmaker attuned to "gaseous perception," or "the pure vision of a non-human eye … an eye which would be in things" (1986, p. 81). But perhaps the most powerful technique involves rejecting the camera altogether, to produce cameraless films, of which *Mothlight* is perhaps most famous.

By way of describing the project of nonhuman vision—his "unprejudiced" eye—Brakhage gestures directly to the project of *Mothlight*: "Speculate as to insect vision such as the bee's sense of scent thru ultraviolet perceptibility. To search for human visual realities, man must, as in all other homo motivation, transcend the original physical restrictions and inherit worlds of eyes" (1963, p. 125). Today, Brakhage's speculation on "insect vision" recalls nothing so much as the project of Speculative Realism, a loose-knit movement in contemporary philosophy united by an effort to de-privilege human subjectivity in favor of more "democratic" notions of realism. Ian Bogost, a scholar occasionally associated with the Speculative Realists, proposes a kind of "alien phenomenology," which explicitly attempts to do precisely what Brakhage suggests—to explore the possibilities of perception by other-than-human entities (2012). Indeed, in an early lecture, Brakhage expresses his desire to access an "alien world beneath the surface of our visibility" (quoted in Hedges 2007, p. 166). Perception, here, is key. Brakhage writes, "there is a pursuit of knowledge foreign to language and founded upon visual communication, demanding a development of the optical mind, and dependent upon perception in the original and deepest sense of the word" (1963, p. 120). "Perception" carries the denotative meaning of a process of awareness through the senses, but Brakhage clearly intends it in a more philosophical sense.[11] Perception, combined with his earlier intent to "inherent worlds of eyes" modifies Merleau-Ponty's phrase, "to see is to have at a distance" (1964, p. 166). In Brakhage's film, particularly his investigation of nonhuman perspectives, implies that to see is to *be* at a distance, that is, to see one of Brakhage's films is to see with eyes, even senses, other than one's own.

Considering Brakhage's suppression of the anthropocentric perspective, it is my argument that *Mothlight* is in fact a true biocentric erasure in the manner of *Darkness*, foregrounding life and subordinating human narrative through the removal (erasure) of the camera. On the launch screen, the Criterion edition of the film includes the following: "What a moth might see from birth to death if black were white and white were black. S.B." (1963). And indeed, Brakhage did use those words to describe *Mothlight*, even as early as *Metaphors on Vision*. What this short phrase makes clear, though, is that the film we are about to see is going to present us with a perspective that is explicitly nonhuman—a kind of moth vision.

---

[11] The *OED* (n.d.) offers this alternative meaning of "perception": "The capacity to be affected by a physical object, phenomenon, etc., without direct contact with it."

In "Affect and Environment: Two Artists' Films and a Video," Sean Cubitt finds in *Mothlight* a meditation on "the personal component of perception and the desire to alter the perceptual habits of wider communities, and in doing so to introduce the possibility of seeing with other eyes, other senses, that are not exclusively human: indeed, *Mothlight* has frequently been interpreted as an account of the moth's perception of her habitat" (2014, p. 257). *Mothlight*, from this perspective, might be viewed in context of "the New Vision" proposed by Lázló Moholy-Nagy in the 1920s, a photographic disruption of human visual experience.

Yet, this film is not merely an alternate perspective but rather a wholesale *inversion* of perspective, given that Brakhage hinges his supposition of moth vision on "if black were white and white were black." *Mothlight* intentionally inverts the typical hermeneutic framework of human visual experience. While, in the normative hierarchy of human perception (and even in one version of Brakhage's story about the creation of *Mothlight*) moths might be anthropomorphized as metaphors for human experience, in *Mothlight* the viewer is, for lack of a better term, *lepidopteromorphized*—endowed with moth-like qualities. Indeed, the short four-minute film that follows allows the viewer to imagine what it would be like to "see" as a moth—a flicker of wings, the texture of grass, crumpled and veiny leaves, bright light, darkness. Like *Darkness*, *Mothlight* exists in a medium that is legible to human perception, what we would typically refer to as a visual medium. Yet, because of their biocentric subject, these works aim to resist a hierarchical ordering of life that positions humanity over other forms of life. Brakhage, in his explicitly biocentric works, insists on the validity of nonhuman perceptual experiences.

But how are we to consider *Mothlight* an erasure? After all, Brakhage did not appropriate a canonical work and physically remove text or image. Yet, *Mothlight* is marked by the same absence as *Darkness*: the absence of human narrative. Narrative, that hallmark of cinema, is conspicuously, constitutively absent from *Mothlight*. But there is a more salient, medialogical erasure evident in Brakhage's method for creating *Mothlight*: the meta-erasure of the camera itself. The camera—in McLuhan's terms, the "extension" of the human eye—has been erased from the filmmaking process. Brakhage writes, "I am after pure film art forms, forms in no way dependent upon imitation of existing arts nor dependent upon the camera used as the eye." By denying himself the most effective visual prosthetic available, Brakhage erases human subjectivity from not only the *content* of the film but also the *form*. The film medium—light plus time—is leveraged here as a device capable of neutralizing the hierarchy of phenomenology that privileges human perceptual experience over all others.

This reading of *Mothlight* runs contrary to much of the critical response to the film over the years. For example, Brakhage had originally intended to title the piece *Dead Spring*, referring to the method of composition (picking up dead leaves, grass, and moth wings) more than the perceptual experience the film produces. Writing on *Mothlight*, P. Adams Sitney writes, "True to that original but inferior title [*Dead Spring*] the film incarnates the sense of the indomitable division between consciousness and nature" (2002, p. 174). Contrary to Sitney's view, my reading of the film explicitly *rejects* the division between consciousness and nature as illusory. In my view, *Mothlight* recognizes that consciousness emerges from and remains within nature. Recall Morrison: "While there is inside there is no outside." While Brakhage's film, like *Darkness*, ultimately fails to provide an "accurate" or otherwise realistic representation of moth vision (which, given the nano-scale technologies available, might be more attainable today), this is precisely not the point. The point of *Mothlight*, its central argument, is that there in fact *are* alternatives to human perception about which we may speculate. By presciently invoking—ten years prior to the foundation of the movement—the biocentric values of deep ecology, Brakhage demonstrates the capacity of film to serve not only as a visual medium but as a physical medium that "contains multitudes" of perceptual experiences, not all of them visual, not all of them human.

3.5 Bewildering the Medium

In 1962, the year before Stan Brakhage released *Mothlight*, Rachel Carson published the now famous environmentalist treatise *Silent Spring* (1962). Immediately, we hear the resonance between Carson's title and Brakhage's original title: *Dead Spring*. Carson, too, it should be noted, devotes a considerable portion of this work detailing the U.S. government's "all-out chemical war on the gypsy moth" (2002, p. 158). It is not all clear that Brakhage had read Carson, or that he was aware of the "1957 Gypsy-Moth Eradication Program" cited in *Silent Spring*. What is abundantly clear is that Carson's central metaphor—a "silent spring," without the noise of flora and fauna—resonates as a critique of anthropocentric "erasure" using pesticides, the advancement of human society at the expense of nonhuman life, putting it in conversation with both Brakhage's *Mothlight* and Morrison's *Darkness*. In the early 1960s, Carson did not yet have the vocabulary to articulate a true biocentrism—the Deep Ecology movement was still ten years away at the time of her writing—but she turned to the closest precedent for biocentric thinking: Albert Schweitzer. Note the dedication page from *Silent Spring*: "To Albert Schweitzer / who said / 'Man has lost the capacity to forsee and forestall. / He will end by destroying the earth'" (2002, p. iv). By dedicating *Silent Spring* to Schweitzer, Carson is implicitly invoking his concept of "Reverence for Life," a nonhierarchical bioethics that is the forerunner of modern biocentrism.[12]

As *Darkness* and *Mothlight* demonstrate, though, any notion of biocentrism must be predicated on an expansion or derangement of sensory perception. Carson knew that the sensory hierarchy separating humans from nonhumans was a powerful ontological distortion, hence her warning of a "silent spring" rather than, perhaps more accurately, an "extinction spring." This simple insight is, in fact, the foundation of wilderness philosophy, which might be summarized as a kind of corrective, immersive "close listening" to nonhuman voices. In a passage that anticipates *Darkness*, the wilderness theorist Max Oelschlaeger writes, "if it is through language that we have been alienated from nature, then reconciliation might also be effected through language" (1992, pp. 271–272). Oelschlaeger's *The Idea of Wilderness* presents a near-comprehensive historical account of humanity's relationship to and perception of "wilderness" from prehistory through postmodern and contemporary perspectives. The central argument guiding Oelschlaeger's study, indeed, most of wilderness philosophy, is that though a truly pure wilderness does not exist, the *idea* of wilderness—a nonhuman otherness—serves as a constructive counterpoint to an anthropocentric view of the world. He writes,

---

[12] In his autobiography, Schweitzer describes a scene not unlike the opening of *Heart of Darkness*: "In that mental state, I had to take a long journey up the river ... Lost in thought, I sat on deck of the barge, struggling to find the elementary and universal concept of the ethical that I had not discovered in any philosophy. I covered sheet after sheet with disconnected sentences merely to concentrate on the problem. Two days passed. Late on the third day, at the very moment when, at sunset, we were making our way through a herd of hippopotamuses, there flashed upon my mind, unforeseen and unsought, the phrase: 'Reverence for Life.' The iron door had yielded. The path in the thicket had become visible. Now I had found my way to the principle in which affirmation of the world and ethics are joined together!" (1949, p. 155).

Human beings are not pure thinking things ensconced within Euroculture but beings whose thoughts and feelings are embodied, centered, in an organic human nature fashioned in the web of life over the longueurs of space and time, internally related to nature. Wilderness experience indelibly conveys the immediate reality of this natural universe of human experience. (1991, p. 9)

In Oelschlaeger's view, ignorance of this fact and neglect of the idea of wilderness produces the kind of resourcism and exploitation that has precipitated and sustained global climate crisis. Only by attending to the idea of wilderness can humanity achieve the kind of "reconciliation" of which Oelschlaeger speaks.

The deep erasure we find in Morrison's *Darkness* is precisely the kind of attempt at reconciliation of which Oelschlaeger speaks. By whiting-out the references to humanity in *Heart of Darkness*, Morrison is not denying humanity its right to speak but merely resisting the human tendency to speak only of ourselves. Not by accident, Morrison chooses the medium of the printed text through which to enact her biocentrism. As Manes writes, "As cultural artifacts, texts embody human (or ostensibly divine) subjects, but stand conspicuously outside nature, whose status as subject therefore becomes problematical in ways unknown to nonliterate, animistic societies" (1992, p. 343). Deep erasure, then, comes to be seen as the denial of the "outside," the reentry of nature into the sphere of discourse as a speaking subject. By attending to the latent, nonhuman narratives left behind after the erasure of references to humanity, *Darkness* becomes, in effect, a simulation of a wilderness experience, facilitating for the reader Oelschlaeger's view of humanity as "internally related to nature" (that is, rather than above or outside) and Morrison's illustration of an "endlessly precarious entanglement." The act of erasure may thus be seen as a kind of abstraction—removing not just references to humanity but the ideological structural supports of anthropocentrism as well. In the framework of *Darkness*, a biocentric erasure is directly opposed to the anthropocentric status quo. Crucially, though, *Darkness* is not merely a statement of these principles but a performance of a wilderness *ethic*, one that comes into sharper relief when we consider the short history of biocentric ethics beginning in the early 1970s with the Deep Ecology movement.

"Deep ecology," writes Oelschlaeger, "presents an idea of wilderness contradictory to resourcism and inconsistent with preservationism since it moves beyond any appeal to instrumental values as a ground for guiding human action" (1991, p. 301). That is, deep ecologists reject all environmentalisms founded upon logic that treat the natural world as a resource to be consumed or preserved. For Deep Ecology, then, value is inherent within the natural world, not relative to human use value. Drawing on the writing of the ostensible founder of Deep Ecology, Arne Naess, Oelschlaeger includes the following table of fundamentals:

DEEP ECOLOGISTS believe that
—all life on earth has intrinsic value
—the richness and diversity of life itself has value
—human life is privileged only to the extent of satisfying vital needs
—maintenance of the richness and diversity of life mandates a decrease in human population
—humankind's relations to the natural world presently endanger the richness and diversity of life
—changes (consistent with cultural diversity) affecting basic economic, technologic, and ideological cultural components are therefore necessary
—"Green societies" value the quality of life (e.g., beauty) more than the quantity of life (e.g., GNP)
—individuals subscribing to these fundamentals of deep ecology are obligated to promote sociocultural change. (1991, p. 303)

As we can see from this table, much of what Oelschlaeger identifies as central to Deep Ecology resonates with the methodology of deep erasure illustrated by Morrison and Brakhage: notably the principle of biocentrism, which corresponds to the first item in Oelschlaeger's table.

To those familiar with Naess's early writings on Deep Ecology, however, Oelschlaeger's list of principles is marked by a conspicuous absence. In the journal *Inquiry* in 1973, Naess published a summary of a lecture he gave to the World Future Research Conference in Bucharest the year before.[13] In this brief piece, Naess attempts to illustrate the distinction between the Deep Ecology that he espouses and what he calls "The Shallow Ecology movement," which is marked by a "Fight against pollution and resource depletion. Central objective: the health and affluence of people in the developed countries" (1973, p. 95). We might recognize

---

[13] According to Peder Anker, Naess's original manuscript only exists in a Romanian translation, the original having been lost (2008, p. 56). Thus, the only record of this lecture we have in English is the *Inquiry* publication, which Naess reconstituted from his notes for the lecture.

"shallow ecology" in the form of today's popular environmentalist movement. In opposition to "shallow ecology," Naess proposes seven characteristics of Deep Ecology, the second of which he calls "*Biospherical egalitarianism*" is defined as follows: "*the equal right to live and blossom*". (1973, p. 96, emphasis in original). While Oelschlaeger's table of the fundamentals of Deep Ecology includes a few statements about the intrinsic value of life, Naess's theory of biospherical egalitarianism is much more explicit. With this concept, Naess insists that all life not only has value but that has *equal* value, a small but significant elaboration lacking from Oelschlaeger's analysis of Deep Ecology.

Though Oelschlaeger's study of the Deep Ecology movement neglects this principle, it has been validated under different terms in contemporary environmental discourse. Manes, for example, advocates what he calls "ecological humility," giving biospherical egalitarianism an evolutionary slant by insisting that "in nature there simply is no higher or lower, first or second, better or worse. There is only the unfolding of life form after life form, more or less genealogically related, each with a mix of characteristics" (1992, p. 342). What would a poetic praxis informed by biospherical egalitarianism look like? I suggest that it would look a good deal like Morrison's *Darkness*. In fact, it becomes clear that this kind of biospherical egalitarianism is central to what I have called deep erasure, the advancement of the principles of Deep Ecology by way of an intervention into the medium of any cultural expression. I suggest that Morrison's effort toward "turning a story into a picture" constitutes a kind of bewilderment, a "making-wild," of the print medium. As I suggested in the previous chapter in context of the debate over textual materialism, an emphasis on the visual (perceptual) qualities of a text can serve as a mediator between textuality (language) and materiality (world: an anthrodecentric category). Deep Erasure embraces the mediation of the visual, actively resisting the anthropocentric hierarchy, bewildering human perception, foregrounding the materiality of the medium. As *Darkness* illustrates, meditating on the idea of wilderness is the most effective method to foreground the notion biospherical egalitarianism. In *Darkness*, we find the emergence of nature as an active subject in the sphere of discourse: "rose, / wilderness," as if to speak, as if to announce its value (2012, p. 98).

3.6 Among the Being of Being

The catalog for an exhibition called "Beyond Nature," by the artist Celina Jeffrey, includes an essay by Levi Bryant, one of the scholars associated with the Speculative Realist movement. In the essay, entitled "Wilderness Ontology," Bryant muses that "wilderness" is perhaps "an adequate name to allude to the being of being" (19). Bryant illustrates how "wilderness" is not in fact a *place* but rather an *ethic*. Bryant concludes,

> the experience of the wilderness at least has the virtue of dislodging the ontological sovereignty of human and bringing us before an experience of beings where we are not lords of a world composed of passive nonhumans, but where we are *among* a variety of different agencies with ends very different than our own and where beings are not simply an object of our regard or gaze, but where we too are objects of the regard or gaze of others. (2011, p. 21)

References

Achebe, Chinua. 2016. An image of Africa: Racism in *heart of darkness*. *The Massachusetts Review* 57: 14–27. https://doi.org/10.1353/mar.2016.0003.

Anderson, Erik. 2006. In the cloud chamber: On Ronald Johnsons's Radi os. *Denver Quarterly* 40 (4): 3–6.

Anker, Peder. 2008. Deep ecology in Bucharest. *The Trumpeter* 24 (1): 56–67. https://trumpeter.athabascau.ca/index.php/trumpet/article/view/1028. Accessed 26 June 2015.

Barad, Karen. 2007. *Meeting the universe halfway: Quantum physics and the entanglement of matter and meaning*. Durham: Duke University Press.

Bogost, Ian. 2012. *Alien phenomenology, or what it's like to be a thing*. Minneapolis: University of Minnesota Press.

Brakhage, Stan. 1963. *Metaphors on vision*. New York: Film Culture.

Brakhage, Stan, Ronald Johnson, and Jim Shedden. 2001. Another way of looking at the universe. *Chicago Review* 47 (4): 31–37. https://doi.org/10.2307/25304800.

Bryant, Levi. 2011. Wilderness ontology. In *Preternatural*, ed. Celina Jeffery, 21–22. Santa Barbara: Punctum Books.

Carson, Rachel. 2002. *Silent spring*. Boston: Mariner. (Original work published 1962).

Connolly, Matthew. 2016. 'But the narrative is not gloomy': Imperialist narrative, blackwood's Edinburgh magazine, and the suitability of *heart of darkness* in

1899. *Victorian Periodicals Review* 49 (1): 76–99. https://doi.org/10.1353/vpr.2016.0004.

Conrad, Joseph. 2008. *Heart of Darkness & The Secret Sharer*. New York: Signet Classics. (Original work published in 1899).

Cubitt, Sean. 2014. Affect and environment in two artists' films and a video. In *Moving environments: Affect, emotion, ecology, and film*, ed. Alexa Weik von Mossner, 249–265. Ontario: Wilfrid Laurier University Press.

Davis, Mike. 2001. *Late Victorian holocausts: El Niño famines and the making of the third world*. New York: Verso.

Deleuze, Gilles. 1986. *Cinema I: The movement-image*. Minneapolis: University of Minnesota Press.

Hawkins, Hunt. 1979. Conrad's critique of imperialism in *heart of darkness*. *PMLA* 94 (2): 286–299. https://doi.org/10.2307/461892.

Hedges, Inez. 2007. Stan Brakhage's film testament: The four Faust films. In *Avant-Garde Film*, ed. Alexander Graf and Dietrich Scheunemann, 165–182. Leiden: Rodopi.

Howe, Susan. 1990. *The Europe of trusts*. New York: New Directions.

———. 2012. The art of poetry no. 97. Interview by Maureen N. McLane. *The Paris Review* 203: 145–169.

Johnson, Ronald. 2005. *Radi os*. Chicago: Flood Editions.

———. 2014. *ARK*. Chicago: Flood Editions.

MacDonald, Travis. 2009. A brief history of erasure poetics. *Jacket* 38. https://jacketmagazine.com/38/macdonald-erasure.shtml. Accessed 4 October 2014.

Manes, Christopher. 1992. Nature and silence. *Environmental Ethics* 14 (4): 339–350. https://doi.org/10.5840/enviroethics19921445.

McCaffery, Steve. 2012. Corrosive poetics: The relief composition of Ronald Johnson's *Radi os*. In *The darkness of the present: Poetics, anachronism, and the anomaly*, 25–40. Tuscaloosa: University of Alabama Presse.

McHale, Brian. 2005. Poetry under erasure. In *Theory into poetry: New approaches to the lyric*, ed. Eva Muller-Zettelman and Margarete Rubik, 277–301. Leiden: Rodopi.

Merleau-Ponty, Maurice, and James M. Edie. 1964. *The primacy of perception: And other essays on phenomenological psychology, the philosophy of art, history, and politics*. Evanston: Northwestern University Press.

Morrison, Yedda. 1998. Integrity: My bold new fragrance. *Tripwire* 1 (1): 41–47.

———. 2009. *Darkness (Chapter 1)*. Little Red Leaves. http://littleredleaves.com/ebooks/darkness.pdf. Accessed 26 June 2024.

———. 2012. *Darkness*. Los Angeles: Make Now Books.

———. 2014a. Darkness statement. YeddaMorrison.com. https://yeddamorrison.com/images/darkness-statement. Accessed 23 June 2014.

———. 2014b. *UB english dept. & hallwalls present Yedda Morrison. Poetics plus and exhibit X fiction*. Buffalo, New York: Hallwalls Contemporary Art Center.

Mothlight. 1963. *Directed by Stan Brakhage*. New York: The Criterion Collection.
Naess, Arne. 1973. The shallow and the deep, long-range ecology movement. *A summary. Inquiry* 16 (1): 95–100. https://doi.org/10.1080/00201747308601682.
OED (*Oxford English Dictionary*). n.d.. https://www.oed.com. Accessed 27 June 2017.
Oelschlaeger, Max. 1991. *The idea of wilderness: From prehistory to the age of ecology*. New Haven: Yale University Press.
———. 1992. *The wilderness condition: Essays on the environment and civilization*. San Francisco: Sierra Club Books.
Perloff, Marjorie. 2004. *Differentials: Poetry, poetics, pedagogy*. Tuscaloosa: University of Alabama Press.
Schweitzer, Albert. 1949. *Out of my life and thought: An autobiography*. New York: Henry Holt.
Selinger, Eric. 1992. 'I composed the holes': Reading Ronald Johnson's *Radi Os*. *Contemporary Literature* 33 (1): 46–73. https://doi.org/10.2307/1208373.
Sharif, Solmaz. 2013. The near transitive properties of the political and poetical: erasure. *Evening Will Come* 28 (1). https://thevolta.org/ewc28-ssharif-p1.html. Accessed 25 June 2015.
Silliman, Ron. 2010. *Poetry written with an eraser*. Poetry Foundation. https://poetryfoundation.org/podcasts/75486/poetry-written-with-an-eraser. Accessed 25 June 2015.
Sitney, P. Adams. 2002. *Visionary film: The American avant-Garde, 1943–2000*. Oxford: Oxford University Press.

CHAPTER 4

Environmental Textuality in the Ambient Web

In this chapter, I turn to the media studies concept of "ambience"—an environmental disruption of figure-ground, text-context binaries—in the poetry of Tan Lin to locate emergent poetics at the center of a theory of textuality for the twenty-first century. Ambience has been part of Tan Lin's poetic project for nearly two decades, despite (or perhaps because of) its definitional slipperiness and fundamental ambiguity. For Lin, a poet often associated with conceptual writing due to the appropriative nature of his poetry, ambience—a kind of immersive textual environmentalism—describes both the inputs and the outputs of his poetic process, blurring boundaries between text and context, author and reader.[1] In particular, this chapter explores the implications of ambience in theories of the network and in media ecology, taking as a case study Lin's work, commonly known as *Heath* but appearing in various forms as *Heath: Plagiarism/Outsource*, *Heath Course Pak*, and *Tan Lin // plagiarism/outsource //, Notes Towards the Definition of Culture //, Untilted Heath Ledger Project //, a history of the search engine //,disco OS*. Synthesizing contemporaneous conceptualizations of ambience from the fields of rhetoric, poetics,

---

[1] Paul Stephens includes Lin's *Seven Controlled Vocabularies* and *Heath* as examples of Conceptual writing in "From the Personal to the Proprietary: Conceptual Writing's Critique of Metadata" and "Vanguard Total Index: Conceptual Writing, Information Asymmetry, and the Risk Society" (2012). However, this chapter subscribes to Judith Goldman's view that Lin's *Heath* is "An appropriative though not a Conceptual work" (2011, n.18).

© The Author(s), under exclusive license to Springer Nature Switzerland AG 2025
T. W. Matteson, *Emergent Poetics*, Modern and Contemporary Poetry and Poetics, https://doi.org/10.1007/978-3-031-70737-7_4

network theory and media studies raises the question of what role media ecology plays in a text such as Lin's *Heath*, the ostensible contents of which are assembled from a variety of sources mediated by the internet. Finally, I argue (following Danny Snelson's analysis of the implications of Actor-Network theory in Lin's text) that *Heath* allows us to conceive of a non-anthropocentric theory of media in which texts, authors, and environments participate in a kind of pluralistic agency. This reading traces the multiplicity of agencies as play in Lin's work, and the ambient networks into which they dissolve.

4.1 Ambience Is a [Medium][2]

This chapter is "about" ambience. I say "about" because any study of ambience necessarily inverts our sense of aboutness. The Oxford English Dictionary traces the etymology of the word "ambience" to the Latin ambīre, meaning "to go about." More precisely, the prefix amb- invokes senses of "on both sides, round, about," and the root verb ī-re means "to go" (*OED* n.d.). Therefore, I might just as easily say, "ambience is about this chapter," in that my words enter a discourse environment that is rich with studies on ambience. True to its definition, ambience is in the air today, providing the context for recent contributions in poetics, rhetoric, and media theory. For example, Timothy Morton's *Ecology Without Nature: Rethinking Environmental Aesthetics* advances a theory of ambient poetics, which is defined as "a materialist way of reading texts with a view to how they encode the literal space of their inscription—if there is such a thing—the spaces between the words, the margins of the page, the physical and social environment of the reader" (2007, p. 3). In the field of rhetoric, Thomas Rickert's *Ambient Rhetoric: The Attunements of Rhetorical Being* explores the ontological nature of rhetoric, arguing that "ambience grants not just a greater but an interactive role to what we typically see as setting or context, foregrounding what is customarily background to rhetorical work and thereby making it material, complex, vital, and, in its own way, active" (2013, p. xv). Media theorists Alexander

---

[2] I borrow Lin's use of brackets to enumerate the various "media" forms embodied by his *Seven Controlled Vocabularies* and enumerated in the book's subtitle: *[AIRPORT NOVEL MUSICAL POEM PAINTING FILM PHOTO HALLUCINATION LANDSCAPE]*. Readers may feel free to substitute other media within these brackets.

Galloway and Eugene Thacker argue that networks are inherently ambient—functioning at scales beyond the purview of individual human subjects (2007, p. 157). And Mark Hansen's *Feed-Forward: On the Future of Twenty-First-Century Media* builds on Galloway and Thacker's work, arguing that twenty-first-century media are ambient or "atmospheric," such that "absolutely no privilege is given to any particular individual or node, to any level or degree of complexity" (2015, p. 2). While the theoretical implications of the above studies are wide-ranging, this chapter focuses on the poet Tan Lin, an author whose exploration of ambience predates all the above studies, and whose work performs, rather than theorizes, a thoroughly environmental, ambient textuality.[3]

In an interview with Chris Alexander, Kristen Gallagher, and Gordon Tapper on the poetry review blog/magazine *Galatea Resurrects*, Tan Lin offers the following timeline to explain the emergence of his Heath Ledger project:

> May 8 2007, contacted by Manuel Brito, requesting ms. for fall 2007 publication.
> Fall 2007, still working on ms.
> January 22, 2008 Heath Ledger dies.
> Most of the book was written after this point, and the bulk of the drafts date from February through late June 2008, so about five months. During this period, 23 drafts were done. Most of the stuff written prior to Heath's death in fall 2007 was discarded. The white out article was recycled from an earlier article, which I had sent to *Artforum*. The earliest material from the Pickwick Arms is the preface to a novel, *Our Feelings Were Made by Hand*. It thus dates earlier.
> Ms. turned in to Danielle Aubert July 14th, 2008.
> Ms. turned into Manuel by Danielle in InDesign. July 16, 2008.
> Book arrives from printers October 2008. (2009a)

This timeline is central to an understanding of what kind of book Tan Lin's *Heath* is and in what ways it enacts a contemporary reading environment. The crucial point to note is that *Heath*, or, rather, "Heath Ledger" the actor and celebrity, played no part in the commission or inception of Lin's work. *A* or *the* text may have existed, but the unpublished text that preceded Heath Ledger's death now serves as vacuum around which the published version of *Heath* orbits: as Lin says, "Most of the stuff written

---

[3] Lin's "Interview for an Ambient Stylistics" was published in 1998.

prior to Heath's death in fall 2007 was discarded" (2009a). In its place, Lin has included screenshots of advertisements, snippets of news, and appropriated blog content from the hours and days after Heath Ledger's death. The relationship detailed above, between the published manuscript and the originally commissioned and now discarded draft, suggests that we think of *Heath* not as a book but as the context of a book that never existed. What remains is, in fact, a collage of screenshots, photocopies, and appropriated online text that Tan Lin was reading as the news broke of Heath Ledger's death (2009a).[4] It is, as Lin writes in *Ambience is a Novel with a Logo*, "a removal made out of everything that was attached to it" (2007a); *Heath* as papier-mâché.

The result of Lin's composition via removal and attachment is a condition he calls "ambience." Ambience, more so than any other conceptual framework or method, has been the subject of Lin's poetic project for nearly two decades. During his career, Lin has characterized ambience variously as "a quasi-architectural awareness," "uninteresting and nonmetaphorical," and even as "blankness" (2012b, 2003, p. 13; 2010). In the essay "Interview for an Ambient Stylistics," published in *Tripwire*, Lin writes, "Poems ought to be endlessly permeable, capable of fitting in every-where they happen to be—not just the seminar room or a book review or Barnes and Noble—[but] decentralized and ethereal, transparent, in the air, hidden from sight, non-programmed, deeply repetitive, and they should be divorced from posing a question or supplying an answer" (1998, p. 37). In these passages, Lin suggests that ambience is profoundly environmental: "content" is subordinate to context.

This is borne out in the structure of *Heath Course Pak*, which is nominally composed of two parts: "Part 1 Samuel Pepys and Plagiarism" and "Part 2 Outsource." It becomes clear that the two sections contain an abundance of overlapping material: indeed, Part 1 appears to be Lin's "foul papers," or a draft of the work, including photocopies of printed text with markings on them and sticky notes covering text to be excised while Part 2 is more akin to a fair copy, featuring a neater, typeset version of much of the text and images from Part 1. By including his process within the book, Lin foregrounds method and source, rather than the finished product. In the second part, Lin provocatively invokes the term

---

[4] In its emphasis on temporality and the reading environment, *Heath* is thematically similar to his project *Bib., Rev. Ed.*, (2007b) in which Lin catalogs everything he reads, with haphazard dates, times, and commentary.

"Outsource," which in the context of *Heath* takes on dual meanings. First, outsource is literal: by appropriating text from the internet, the *source* is *out*side of himself: an out-source, rather than an in-source. The second usage is more provocative, calling into question the ethics of the labor involved in typesetting his original notes for the book. Lin's invocation of outsourcing calls to mind Nick Thurston's *Of the Subcontract, or, Principles of Poetic Right* (2013), a collection of 100 poems composed by poorly compensated subcontractors hired through Amazon Mechanical Turk, a web-based platform for digital labor. Both Lin's *Heath*, as an ambient text with multiple credited and uncredited human authors, and Thurston's text, perform outsourcing as form of "pseudocomplicity" (to use Jennifer Scappettone's term), laying bare the contingencies of digital labor and the questionable practices and processes involved in digital production. Both Lin and Thurston, then, regard the method of production as a "text" equally as rich and consequential as the linguistic content of the work.

Lin's ambient work responds to a condition we might call the tyranny of content, whereby a reader willfully ignores, neglects, or otherwise obscures the qualities and contexts of the work that do not readily submit to hermeneutic interpretation. But ambience, for Lin, is not merely about the poem's relationship to its environment but about the poem's emergence from the environment and its status as a simulated environment. It is this latter condition, the poem as environment, that best characterizes Lin's *Heath*. While the content of the text does originate from Lin's own reading environment, which is evidently a web browser, ushering, as he says, "from the things around us and not the things inside us," we cannot lose sight of the poem/book itself, and the experience of reading it, as an environment in its own right (1998, p. 38).

Lori Emerson calls *Heath* "a metawork—a work about the larger network within which it is nested and upon which it depends" (2014, p. 181). If *Heath* is a metawork, then ambience should be seen as a kind of metamedium throughout Lin's work, as he calls it, "today's cultural operating system" (2008, p. 96). But how can a book, otherwise devoid of content, be composed of the "things around" it? This seems to point to the dissolution of the codex as a medium or container, signaled by the improbably long and overlapping subtitles on the cover of the book.[5] In "The

---

[5] Danny Snelson suggests that these apparent subtitles are in fact comma separated values (CSV), part of an imaginary programming language, each subtitle "a useful metadata value for processing the heterogeneous materials in the book" (2010).

Authorship of Heath Ledger in the New Reading Environment; On Tan Lin's *Heath: Plagiarism/Outsource*," Kristen Gallagher writes of "the book's inability to contain its own material, its relationship to some larger space outside itself" (2010, p. 703). In fact, as the above timeline of publication indicates, Lin's revision of the original work into what would become *Heath* subordinates anything resembling "content," foregrounding instead a large collection of material appropriated from the web which Lin collected in the days and weeks following Heath Ledger's death.[6]

From this perspective, *Heath* resembles an mp3 file "containing" John Cage's famous "silent" composition, *4:33*.[7] One would think that any recording of this silent composition would resemble any other, but that perspective would willfully foreclose on ambient intrusions. Silence, of course, is merely a durational medium composed of ambient noise (Cage 2010, p. 80). And the absence of intentionally composed content does not presume the absence of aleatorical or spontaneous external interruptions. As Cage writes, "The mind may be used either to ignore ambient sounds … Or the mind may give up its desire to improve on creation and function as a faithful receiver of experience" (2010, p. 32). Compare Lin's view that *Heath* is a "process of blind labor … whose product is attention, where attention produces the objects that interest us" (2009a).

Though the logic of experimental music does not translate perfectly to digital textuality, the Heath Ledger of Lin's *Heath* is functionally analogous to Cage's theory of silence: a causative absence that presents an opportunity for the author/reader to participate in and gather a heterogeneous collection of ambient "noise" or textual detritus. Lin says, "Heath: he exists as a kind of format-dependent scanning, as does the work itself" (2009a). As a durational metamedium, ambience in *Heath* emerges with "time stamps," both in the ancillary material like the timeline reproduced above and in the de facto "content" of *Heath*, marked with rigorous specificity.[8] Lin writes that this temporal marking "gives a loose, porous conduit: documentary, narrative, affective, etc., for the material and provides a kind of parameter for the particular environment in question where both

---

[6] And growing: Lin seems to be continually revising *Heath*. Later editions, published as *Heath Course Pak* by Counterpath Press, include not only the original "text" but also such paratextual materials as interviews and commentary on the first edition of *Heath*.

[7] Lin cites Cage in *BlipSoak01* (2003, p. 13, n. 1).

[8] This emphasis on temporality is evident in Lin's earlier work, *Blipsoak01*, but instead of marking the date and time of composition, Lin's temporal markers in *Blipsoak01* take the form of durational labels, estimating the time each section would take to read.

the figure and ground are in continual motion" (2009a). Thus, the subject or content of the work is subordinated to the temporal qualities: "this can be read in two or three hours or 'two or three days' max" (2012a).

Ambience, in *Heath* and elsewhere in Lin's oeuvre, is, from this perspective, a primarily durational metamedium of attention, a temporally contingent inversion of content and context such that "figure and ground are in continual motion." But even though ambience figures prominently in both Lin's creative work and the associated interviews, it remains undertheorized in the scholarship on Lin's work. And the lone study exclusively devoted to the issue of ambience in Lin's work, Jennifer Scappettone's "Versus Seamlessness: Architectonics of Pseudocomplicity in Tan Lin's Ambient Poetics" (2009), though it does chart the foundations of ambience in Lin's earlier work, was published prior to the release of *Heath*.

This chapter endeavors both to situate *Heath* within this limited scholarly context as an instance of ambient poetry and to pursue the implications of ambience—manifest in *Heath*—in reconfiguring our understanding of institutional critique, media ecology, and network theory. Ultimately, I will explore the curiously inverted relationship between ambience and emergent poetics, arguing that a radically environmental poetics depends wholly on emergence as its operational mechanism. To make this argument, I must situate *Heath* in context of Lin's earlier work, particularly *BlipSoak01*, *Ambience is a Novel With a Logo*, and *Seven Controlled Vocabularies*,[9] elaborating one of the most consequential implications of ambience in *Heath*: the suppression of institutional critique and the dispersal of agency, both human and nonhuman.

4.2 Some Sort of Plagiarized Accounting

Lin says of *Heath*, "'this' work is Nominally a novel inside a Network" (2012a). As I have discussed above, the online discussion surrounding the event of Heath Ledger's death constitutes the network out of which the "novel" *Heath* emerges. Paradoxically, however, Lin's emphasis on ambience allows us to read *Heath* not only as "a novel inside a Network" but as a network inside of a novel, since the "content" of the work is its environment ("everything that was attached to it"). As Danny Snelson writes

---

[9] The full title is *Seven Controlled Vocabularies and Obituary 2004. The Joy of Cooking [AIRPORT NOVEL MUSICAL POEM PAINTING FILM PHOTO HALLUCINATION LANDSCAPE]* by Tan Lin.

in "*Heath*, Prelude to Tracing the Actor as Network," *Heath* "enacts a heterogeneous network between these previously (seemingly) disparate texts" (2010). But while *Heath* both emerges from a Network—the social network of online discourse—and appropriates the contents of this network to, in Snelson's words, enact a new, "heterogeneous network," we must also read *Heath* in context of another, ancillary network: that of Lin's previous work and the relevant scholarship thereof. One might even argue that this material—all of Lin's previous publications, and all the critical articles written about them—are part of the contents of *Heath*, insofar as its ambient nature makes it the work of the critic not to determine what is inside/outside of the work but to explore all possible threads of connection. As Danny Snelson notes, each of Lin's works is part of a larger poetic project: "every new book for Lin is a form of autobiography, or an exploration of the author's affective experience with textual culture."

The publication of *BlipSoak01* in 2003 marks Tan Lin's first book-length attempt at a poetics of ambience. As Brian Kim Stefans notes in "Streaming Poetry," Lin's BlipSoak01 attempts "to shake off the trappings of the avant-garde—linguistic difficulty, the suspicion of beauty, all manners of formal estrangement—in order to create poems that are 'relaxing'" (2004).

Stefans borrows the idea of relaxation from Lin himself, who suggests that ambient works must put aside the shock aesthetic of the avant-garde and, implicitly, the institutional critique such an aesthetic represented (2009b). Scappettone writes, "Tan Lin's urbane investigation of the poetics of virtuality may constitute the next logical step away from architectonics (and activist shock tactics) as we have known them" (2009, p. 68). But what of the text of *BlipSoak01* itself? To what extent does it achieve this relaxation of the avant-garde? The text begins with a short prose section entitled "Preface." Below this heading appears "Duration [11:03]," presumably the time Lin estimates one should spend reading the preface (and anticipating the "time stamps" in the appropriated material from *Heath*). The Preface amounts to a kind of soft manifesto of ambient poetry in which Lin enumerates a poetics project of inattention, distraction, relation, and boredom.

The Preface, and the poem itself to follow, perform ambience in its unconventional printing methods. In the Preface, text only appears on the recto, or right-hand page, with the except of a handful of words or phrases that spill over onto the verso (left-hand page). In *BlipSoak01*, Lin writes, "The beautiful book should not be read but merely looked at. The boring page makes us wait a very long time. // Everyone likes to // wait, though not in any particular order, for a mistake or an accident. [That is why] the left hand side of the page remains temporarily uninteresting" (2003, pp. 10–11).[10] The poem itself reverses the Preface's layout, as most of the text begins on the verso and occasionally spills across to the recto. These unconventional layouts amount to Lin's gentle disruption of conventional reading practices, drawing attention to surface rather than conceptual or linguistic depth: "the surface of the ambient poem you are now gazing towards is highly distracting" (2003, p. 11). As Jennifer Scappettone notes, such a page layout is designed to prevent the kind of absorption we associate with reading a conventional printed page: "The experience of being engrossed is more troubling than this" (2009, p. 73). That is, Lin's emphasis on ambience subverts the experience of depth and immersion perpetuated by conventional print media.

The title of the work itself gestures to the tension between being distracted and engrossed while reading: Stefans glosses "blip soak" as "information free fall." But a closer look at the word "blip" further illustrates Lin's concern with ambience. According to the *Oxford English Dictionary*, the word "blip" is of echoic origin, an onomatopoeic rendering of a "quick popping sound," which has come to be associated with small marks on a radar screen, in figurative usage "something which is insignificant or attracts little attention" (*OED* n.d.). In the word's resonance with abrupt sonic intrusions and with insignificance, Lin gestures to the paradoxical nature of ambient poetry: to be in the midst of a "blip soak" is to be, essentially, engrossed by distraction. He writes, "The most beautiful page makes you look away accidentally from what you were reading" (2003, p. 13).[11] Crucially, Lin elaborates, "Poems should be uninteresting and non-metaphorical enough to be listened to in passing or while 'thinking of something else'" (2003, p. 13). The suppression of metaphor as fuel for distraction further illustrates the mechanism of the "blip soak," an emphasis on surface and environment, rather than on linguistic content, refusing the immersive leap from vehicle to tenor. The "blip soak," as defined above, strikingly resonates with Lin's compositional process for *Heath*:

[10] Danny Snelson suggests using "//" to denote when Lin's text jumps the gutter from recto to verso and vice versa.

[11] In a footnote affixed to this line, Lin includes (without commentary) the names of some thirty writers and artists, presumably those Lin associates with this kind of ambient writing, ranging from Oscar Wilde to one of Lin's contemporaries, Juliana Spahr.

> The choice of material is directly coded to something I personally connected with at a very specific moment. It was a mild intrusion or a barely noticed break or dilation or evanescence or hyperbole that I was interested in, in an overall ambient environment of which I was a part of, so it would be hard for me to say the interest was "mine." But my being there had to be there; it was the initial starting point and it was about interest, but it was also about the environment that generates interest. (2009a)

Lin's description of "a barely noticed break or dilation or evanescence or hyperbole" is nearly identical to the above understanding of a "blip," foregrounding ambient environmental interruption instead of authorial intention or "content" per se.

Having cemented his departure from the shock aesthetic of avant-garde poetry in *BlipSoak01*, Lin takes on another literary form, the novel, in *Ambience is a Novel with a Logo*, a shorter work published by Katalanche Press in 2007. Though it seems to contain more overtly "autobiographical" material than *BlipSoak01*, *Ambience is a Novel with a Logo* similarly contains a series of aphorisms commenting on the author's beliefs regarding the intended reception of the work in question. Lin writes, "I believe a novel should not preserve things, it should blank them out very very slowly around all those beautiful, corrosive things that are not happening in the world and that usually involve figures of state and violent incursions in countries far from our own and the loss of our loved ones" (2007a). This resonates with Lin's compositional method of attachment via removal in *Heath*. In *BlipSoak01*, Lin indicted "most literature and especially poetry" as "fundamentally false forms of excitation and dread" (2003, p. 16–17). In *Ambience is a Novel with a Logo*, he elaborates: "Every novel is just a form of false advertising, a kind of fragile corporate monogram for something that has not yet become 'dated' or 'historic' or ugly enough" (2007a) And yet, as Scappettone writes, Lin's purpose is not to stage a resistance to and critique of the culture industry but to engage in a kind of "pseudocomplicity with the increasingly total mediation and administration of space as it maneuvers to transform the book into 'a non-branded reading environment'" (2009, p. 73).

The "reading environment" of *Ambience is a Novel with a Logo* is punctuated with images and footnotes seemingly at random, culled, apparently from Google searches and web advertisements Lin encountered during the composition of the main text. For example, a footnote on the first page of the text reads, "32 Consumer Rust Prevention and Rust Removal

Products // The Bull Frog Motorcycle Cocoon actually contains our powerful Rust Blocker to protect your beautiful machine from rust and corrosion over time by" (2007a). In the original text, the footnote maintains its original web formatting and font, foreshadowing the ambient citationality which produces Lin's *Heath*. But the resonances between *Heath* and *Ambience is a Novel with a Logo* are not limited to these formal qualities. In one passage, *Ambience is a Novel with a Logo* seems to anticipate, perhaps too accurately, the emergence of *Heath*: "To keep things more or less straight our family should have kept some sort of plagiarized accounting, part family ledger, photogram album, Huck Finn inventory, design manual, encyclopedia of the not-yet dead. Or scrapbook" (2007a). The litany of media forms—ledger, album, inventory, manual, encyclopedia—resonates with Lin's continued effort to realize a kind of media degree zero, such that the difference between these ambient forms is indistinguishable—"One could go in and out of a book without knowing precisely where one was in it" (2007a). And yet, the apparently coincidental pairing of the words "plagiarized" and "ledger" cannot help but call to mind Lin's *Heath: Plagiarism/Outsource*, even though Heath Ledger was alive when *Ambience is a Novel with a Logo* was published.

In a longer passage appended to a phrase I quoted above, Lin also appears to gesture toward another then-forthcoming publication, signaling that each of his publications participate in the same poetic project: a deep methodological commitment to ambient context. The passage reads:

> One could go in and out of a book without knowing precisely where one was in it. The language would function like a carpet or escalator within the text itself. Craft would be replaced with the handicrafts and the utensils of writing. Thus, recipes, obituaries, receipts, tickets, text messages, itineraries, legal briefs, and disclaimers would constitute various surface entrances. The text would be small and uncontrollable and would accommodate the general flow of the masses. (Lin 2007a)

In addition to the aspiration of accommodating "the general flow of the masses," the references to recipes and obituaries in above passage seem to reference the media-convergence of what would become Lin's *Seven Controlled Vocabularies and Obituary 2004. The Joy of Cooking. [AIRPORT NOVEL MUSICAL POEM PAINTING FILM PHOTO HALLUCINATION LANDSCAPE]*. This work is Lin's most comparable work to *Heath*, as both works feature unconventional metadata tags on their covers, and both consist largely of appropriated text and images.

In "From the Personal to the Proprietary: Conceptual Writing's Critique of Metadata," Paul Stephens writes, "By emphasizing the metadata protocols of the book as physical object, Lin subverts the unit of the poetry book, and by extension places poetry within a far wider discursive field" (2012, par. 12). As Stephens notes, Lin is not simply parodying the contemporary fixation on the convergence of media forms into a single digital medium but emphasizing his own project's attempt to extend beyond its own borders (2012). Lin's emphasis on the ambient convergence of media forms—going "in and out of a book without knowing precisely where one was in it"—attempts to account for the instability of the book as form. In this way, Lin resists the idea of the book as a container, to the extent that the ostensible "contents" of a book cannot be contained by the binding of the book and usher from the book's context rather that from the mind of a single author.

Stephens cites Dan Visel, who says of *Seven Controlled Vocabularies*, "A book is not a text. It's more than a text. It's a text and a collection of information around that text, some of which we consciously recognize and some of which we don't" (quoted in Stephens 2012, par. 12). Visel's assertion seems to point to the limits of established hermeneutic practice, which ignores those qualities and context of media that are not immediately engrossing to the human sensorium and that, consequently, resist interpretation.[12] Compare Visel's redefinition of the book with Vanessa Place's definition of ambience in a review of Lin's *Insomnia and the Aunt*: "Ambience: that which we, in our distraction, fail to register but are certainly affected/afflicted by" (2011). And Kristen Gallagher writes that *Heath* is made up of "the kind of language and framing of language that we tend not to pay attention to" (2010, p. 707). But what is at stake here is not merely raising awareness of the linguistic detritus of the internet. Rather, what Lin's ambient work makes evident is that attention itself is often an anthropocentric medium. From *Heath*: "An attention span produces the things that interest us and not the other way around." And as the trajectory from *Blipsoak01* to *Heath* makes clear, Lin's development of the concept of ambience in his poetry is deeply invested in disrupting the

---

[12] Visel's attention to the para- and extra-textual aspects of a book should be read in contrast to Walter Benn Michaels's argument in *The Shape of the Signifier*, which I address in Chap. 1.

normal protocols of attention, in making a more accurate accounting of the environmental aspects of texts, particularly those aspects which we do not "consciously recognize" (in Visel's terms).

4.3 Against Resistance

One of the more successful attempts at performing such an accounting of Lin's work is Danny Snelson's "*Heath*: Prelude to Tracing the Actor as Network," (2010) which has been collected in Brian Kim Stefans's web-based *Introduction to Electronic Literature: A Freeware Guide*. Snelson's methodology in his analysis of Lin's *Heath* is deeply informed by Actor-Network Theory; in fact, he argues, "any reading of Heath necessarily assumes an actor-network approach" (2010). Actor-Network Theory—in the words of one of its founders and most prominent practitioners, Bruno Latour—is essentially a social methodology for tracing agency in a network of associations. In *Reassembling the Social: An Introduction to Actor-Network Theory*, Latour describes the goals of Actor-Network Theory as follows: "Action is not done under the full control of consciousness; action should rather be felt as a node, a knot, and a conglomerate of many surprising sets of agencies that have to be slowly disentangled" (2005, p. 44). The process of "disentangling" agencies is, as anyone familiar with Latour's work knows, antithetical to what has come to be known as negative or institutional critique.

Despite Latour's growing influence in the world of literary criticism in the last decade, and despite Lin's documented interest in Latour's work,[13] some scholars continue to read *Heath* and Lin's other ambient works in context of the conventional paradigm of institutional critique. For example, in "Vanguard Total Index: Conceptual Writing, Information Asymmetry, and the Risk Society," Paul Stephens characterizes *Heath* as an example of Conceptual writing, saying, "Institutional critique is among the most important concerns of conceptual art and writing" (2013, p. 755). Yet, even though Stephens insists on this characterization—indeed, in an earlier essay Stephens calls *Seven Controlled Vocabularies* a Conceptual work as well—he acknowledges a certain incongruity between Conceptual writing and Lin's work regarding the emphasis on

---

[13] In the Ubuweb edition of Lin's *Bib.*, a record of everything he read from January 10, 2006, to October 31, 2007, there are 12 records of Lin reading Latour.

institutional critique.[14] He writes, "rather than attempting a direct attack on mass culture, attempts something of a sneak attack" (2013, p. 766). In other words, and in large part due to his insistence that Lin is a Conceptualist, Stephens seems to interpret Lin's theory of ambience as critique in disguise.

However, following Actor-Network theory, I suggest that Lin resists easily assigning blame and attributing agency to a single entity. As Lin's own writing makes clear, an "attack," however sneaky, is antithetical to his ambient project, which he regularly describes as "relaxing."[15] Danny Snelson highlights "the various critical misunderstandings around *Heath*—how can Lin write critically about (and through) the very relaxing, ambient systems it compares itself to: RSS feeds, shopping, dining in a restaurant" (2010). In fact, as Snelson has noted, Lin's project is much closer to Latour's vision of disentangling agencies than institutional critique, by embedding his work within, rather than outside or against, the various discursive environments in which Lin is interested—a condition which Jennifer Scappettone calls "pseudocomplicity" (2009). By this term, Scappettone intends to characterize investigations in ambient as "contemporary poetry's reaction to the dampening of sociohistorical contradictions" (2009, p. 64). Such a step is roughly in line with Lin's attempt to shift away from a confrontational avant-garde toward ambience and relaxation: "the next logical step away from architectonics (and activist shock tactics) as we have known them" (Scappettone 2009, p. 68). If Lin's ambient poetry steps away from shock tactics, what is it moving toward? Scappettone argues that Lin's departure from these tactics—and, by extension, institutional critique—"mimics the way the culture industry performs today so that viewers of it can glean, however vaguely or inadvertently, some recognition of what's happening (and what's not) in other sectors of cultural dissemination" (2009, p. 75). In this way, Lin's work constitutes not a critique but a simulation that partly parodies and partly attunes the reader to the dissemination and reception of various forms of ambient language in a digitally mediated reading environment.

Likewise, in an article analyzing the prominence of the logic of search engines in Lin's work, Lori Emerson characterizes Lin as a kind of participant-observer in the various systems *Heath* simulates. She argues, "Lin's

---

[14] See Paul Stephens's "From the Personal to the Proprietary: Conceptual Writing's Critique of Metadata."

[15] See Lin's "Ambience is a Novel with a Logo," 38.

primary motive in placing Google at the center of the production process for *HEATH* is more to observe the googlization of everything than to ... critique" (2008, p. 182). To observe rather than to critique means setting aside revelatory claims of social construction and taking up the tools of Actor-Network theory to trace the complicated associations in a mediated environment. Emerson writes, "Lin's interest seems to lie more in bringing to the fore his own readingwriting practice at the level of a user/consumer of Google's engine than in drawing attention to the constructedness of the search engine" (2008, p. 182). That is, rather than turning to the tired critique that Google's search algorithm is not neutral—that Google skews page rankings—Lin explores the influence of the search engine on his own reading and writing life.[16] In doing so, Lin appears to be advocating for the creative misuse of Google, rather than a wholesale rejection of it based on its problematic institutional ideological standards.

In another interview, Chris Alexander, whose name appears listed as one of the "co-authors" on the rear cover of *Heath Course Pak*, describes his own poetic practice similarly.

Referring to *Panda*, his appropriative work devoted to the animated film *Kung Fu Panda*, Alexander says in an interview with Kristen Gallagher and Christopher Schmidt that he was committed to

> not engaging in negative critique. Which I feel is something that is very important to me at the moment, in the wake of Language poetry. Since the early nineties in particular, American poetry has been sort of reflexively caught up in this moment of negative critique. It's an assumed thing that you're engaging in a spirit of critical distance and a kind of Marxist-inflected scrutiny.
>
> Whereas in this project what I was wanting to do was occupy this space of—I was thinking I could learn just as much about these commercial processes by attempting to enter into them in spirit, instead of standing apart from them and critiquing them. In some ways what the book really tries to do is become an extension of the *Kung Fu Panda* franchise in a way. It's sort of an archeology of the franchise, but it's also an illicit entry into the franchise. A *Kung Fu Panda* knockoff, like the poetry edition. (2012)

Helpfully, Alexander historicizes this commitment as an intentional shift away from what we might call "paranoid writing" (after Eve Sedgwick's

---

[16] See for example Eric Goldman's "*Search Engine Bias and the Demise of Search Engine Utopianism*" (2006).

notion of paranoid reading) in the critical mode toward a more ambient poetics.[17] Instead of "problematizing" *Kung Fu Panda*'s culturally appropriative nature, its dependence on racial stereotypes deflected halfheartedly by anthropomorphic talking animals, Alexander's *Panda* inhabits the film franchise and the cultural industry surrounding it, aiming at understanding cultural phenomena rather than revealing so-called hidden ideologies.

Like Alexander's project, Lin's work—and *Heath* in particular—similarly relinquishes the kind of critical distance that Alexander associates with the innovative poetries of the 1990s and early 2000s. Yet, unlike Alexander's *Panda*, Lin's *Heath* is less committed to participating in any one particular "commercial process" (such as a film franchise) and more invested in a kind of meta-simulation of a digital communication environment, of which his parody/participation in "outsourcing" is but one aspect. While both *Panda* and *Heath* are nominally "about" Hollywood icons—an animated panda and a human actor—*Heath* is less of a subject heading than a temporal contingency, a motivating absence. What sets *Heath* apart is not its turn away from negative critique but precisely what it turns toward: an emphasis on agency. While it is true that a commitment to "Actor-Network Theory signals the exhaustion of critique, it also offers an affirmative method: a multifarious inquiry launched with the tools of anthropology, philosophy, metaphysics, history, sociology to detect how many participants are gathered in a thing to make it exist and to maintain its existence" (Latour 2004, p. 246). In "Interview for an Ambient Stylistics," Lin puts it this way: "A perfect poet ... would do nothing every day except use as many words as she or he could to count things" (1998, p. 35). Strikingly, both Latour and Lin emphasize a quantitative methodological approach: "to detect how many," "to count things." This consonance suggests that Lin's project (and the Actor-Network Theory undergirding it) is not only engaged in pseudocomplicity but is invested in showing that action is complex, the product of an assemblage and not solely attributable to individual human actors.

The degree to which *Heath* succeeds at this project depends on just such a reconceptualization of agency to account for the agency of

---

[17] See Eve Kosofsky Sedgwick, "Paranoid Reading and Reparative Reading, or, You're So Paranoid, You Probably Think This Essay Is About You."

nonhumans.[18] In "Actor-Network Theory and Methodology: Just What Does it Mean to Say that Nonhumans Have Agency?" Edwin Sayes argues that Actor-Network Theory "presents a coherent methodology for incorporating nonhumans into social scientific accounts" (2014, p. 135). Sayes carefully defines nonhumans as, essentially, any *thing*—excluding humans, supernatural entities, symbols, and assemblages of humans and nonhumans (2014, p. 136). Tuning in to nonhumans, in context of *Heath*, indicates that Lin's project is interested in rethinking the boundary between actor and network, rather than simply rethinking the *relationship* between an actor and a network. In an essay entitled "Disco as Operating System, Part One," which appeared roughly contemporaneously to *Heath*, Lin makes precisely this point, associating the dissolution of boundaries between actor and network with disco music. He writes,

> disco is not principally a commodity pressed on vinyl and consumed in a rec room, but a cultural format accessed in a communal setting where the line between singing and acting, listening and participating, between a celebrity and what Warhol called a "nobody," and between an individual and a network were being dissolved. (2008, p. 84)

Lin puts this in context of *Heath* in his interview for *Galatea Resurrects*: "The particular environment in question where both the figure and ground are in continual motion" (2009a). "Figure" and "individual," from this perspective, are obsolete fictions; no longer can these terms be used to associate agency with subjective intentionality.

What remains is, in the view of Actor-Network Theory, an analysis that begins with a fundamental uncertainty about who or what is exercising agency. As Sayes writes, "ANT, in fact, attempts to pluralize what it means to speak of agency … decoupled from criteria of intentionality, subjectivity, and free-will" (2014, p. 141). Hence, the "Tan Lin" of the spine and cover of *Heath* is not an author but rather "a useful metadata value for processing the heterogeneous materials in the book" (Snelson 2010). "Tan Lin" is one of many, including the subtitles—*plagiarism/outsource //, Notes Towards the Definition of Culture //, Untitled Heath Ledger Project //, a history of the search engine //, disco OS*—and the names of

---

[18] In this chapter, I follow Actor-Network theory in considering nonhumans within complex assemblages, a perspective which pluralizes agency and draws a sharp distinction between agency and intentionality.

"co-authors" on the rear cover—Amazon Turk, Kristen Gallagher, Gordon Tapper, Danny Snelson, Ina Luem, Michael Lee, Sooyoung Lee, Jennifer Tsuei, Helena Zhang, Tamido Beyer, Jean Sung, Danielle Aubert, Tim Roberts. The pluralization of authorship in *Heath*—including both humans and nonhuman-human assemblages—reflects one of the crucial characteristics of nonhuman agency. According to Sayes, "nonhumans do not have agency by themselves, if only because they are never by themselves" (2014, p. 144). And, given that Actor-Network Theory rejects the human–nonhuman binary, we can extrapolate that agency cannot be attributed exclusively to human individuals either.

Such a position must radically reconfigure both the social sciences and political theory, which Sayes and others, including and especially Bruno Latour, address at length elsewhere.[19] My aim, however, is to trace the implications of the pluralization of agency for textual practices in the digital age, following Lin's *Heath* as a kind of meta-text. Sayes frames consequences of this shift in the attribution of agency rather modestly:

> The perspective asks that we remain open to the possibility that nonhumans add something that is of sociological relevance to a chain of events: that something happens, that this something is added by a nonhuman, and that this addition falls under the general rubric of action and agency. It is the action itself that is the important thing to trace ... An a priori distinction between the agential capacities of humans and nonhumans ceases to be helpful if it acts to occlude, to stack our accounting enterprises before we have even commenced counting. (2014, p. 145)

In its suppression of subject–object/human–nonhuman hierarchies, the above passage indicates that we should include nonhuman agencies in Lin's method of the "perfect poet" whose goal should be "to count things." Phrased another way, we might say that for Lin, *things count*, that nonhumans matter, that (in Sayes's words) "something is added," and this additive capacity is a difference which we can call agency.

In "*Heath*: Prelude to Tracing the Actor as Network," Danny Snelson briefly invokes nonhumans in context of Lin's *Heath*. Explicating one of the subtitles of the work—*Notes Towards the Definition of Culture*—Snelson turns to the T. S. Eliot essay of the same title to explore the

---

[19] See for example Bruno Latour, *An Inquiry into Modes of Existence: An Anthropology of the Moderns* (2012).

reasons for Lin's invocation of it. Snelson turns to the following passage in that original essay to point to Eliot's definition of culture as inclusive of:

> all the characteristic activities and interests of a people: Derby Day, Henley Regatta, Cowes, the 12th of August, a cup final, the dog races, the pin table, the dart board, Wensleydale cheese, boiled cabbage cut into sections, beetroot in vinegar, 19th-century Gothic churches and the music of Elgar. The reader can make his own list. (qtd. in Snelson 2010)

Snelson notes that culture, in Eliot's view, is largely composed of nonhumans, something that he claims would "delight the actor-network theorist" (2010). Snelson then moves perhaps too quickly past the implications of nonhuman agency in Lin's work, saying, "Lin, however, who often works with similarly extensive and incongruous lists … might be most interested in the final line commanding the reader's autonomy" (2010). Yet, considering Lin's suppression (and outsourcing) of authorship in *Heath*, in the way in which so much of the work arises from the author's reading environment rather than from the author's intention, the term "autonomy" may be an exaggeration. Later, Snelson himself analogizes that Lin as author represents the "actor as computational device"; the actor/author, therefore, does not exist in isolation but merely acts as an organizational protocol, an information-aggregating program that depends on both humans and nonhumans for its function (2010).

If nonhumans are essential for a full actor-network accounting, then they are essential for any reading of *Heath*. As Sayes writes, "the actions and capacities of nonhumans that are seen as a condition for the possibility of the formation of human society" (2014, p. 137). Three acronyms that feature prominently in *Heath* illustrate the function of nonhumans as just such "a condition of possibility" structures that shape the contours of human society: RSS, GSM, and GNU. These acronyms constitute both "individual" nonhumans—as digital media composed of circuitry and code—and networks that bring together both humans and nonhumans, appearing as logoed references within *Heath*. RSS—Rich Site Summary—serves as both a literal aid in the composition of *Heath* (pushing news alerts and commentary on Heath Ledger's death to Lin's computer) and as analogous to *Heath*'s own "volatile" format as composed of diverse source material and dispersed in a variety of formats and editions (*Galatea* interview). As the name suggests, GSM, the Global System for Mobile Communication, is the predominant cellular network worldwide, connecting billions of people and devices. As Lin notes, "Heath, the actor's (death), is experienced over the phone. Consciousness belongs to the environment, regarded as a system of differentiated communication platforms, one of which might be literature" (2009a). The final acronym, GNU, is a recursive acronym that stands for "GNU's not UNIX." That is, GNU is essentially a free and open-source operating system like the proprietary commercial UNIX operating system. In *Heath*, the GNU logo appears directly below the phrase "a cloud data bank" (Lin 2012a). Like RSS and GSM, GNU exists as an "individual" composed of computer code; as a network GNU unites users, software (including cloud services), and computing objects like servers and desktop computers.

These nonhumans are perhaps the predominant "conditions of possibility for the formation of human society" today as they facilitate the dominant forms of digitally mediated communication and language transmission. And their presence in *Heath*, both as visual references, procedural composition tools, and analogies for the book's "final" form indicates that attunement to nonhuman agency is essential for Tan Lin's ambient poetics. It will be important to note, however, that these acronyms refer to operations at a variety of scales: at a microcosmic level, each acronym refers to an individual piece of computer code, but at from a macrocosmic level, these protocols constitute networks in their own right, connecting data, humans, and devices. At an even greater scale, we can see that RSS, GSM, and GNU not only constitute individual autonomous networks but also belong to the same informational network that includes cell towers, ISPs, weather patterns, and topographical features in addition to human users and other nonhuman entities. This scalar complexity demonstrates the impossibility of standing outside such a network to critique it, hence Lin's emphasis on both pseudocomplicity and a post-critical ambient engagement.

4.4 Exteriorizing the Ecosystem

Nonhumans exert their influence on *Heath* primarily as networked and networking phenomena, making it impossible to account for isolated individual agencies. In this way, accounting for the nonhuman agency in *Heath* validates Lin's description of the work as "a novel inside a Network" (2012a). But, as "networks" themselves, the nonhuman presences in *Heath* make it clear that we could equally regard the work as a "Network inside a novel." The fundamental shift here is that the distinction between inside and outside is no longer immediately apparent, nor is it—as we shall see—accurate. As Lin says in an interview with *Bomb* magazine, "Context is more important than content ... Every book is an abbreviation/revision that erects some sort of false distinction or difference between reading and nonreading, between the life lived inside and the life outside the book. I wanted to exteriorize the ecosystem of reading as much as possible" (2010). For Lin, as we have seen, the immersive nature of traditional reading practices constructs the illusion of individual subjectivity, raising false barriers between and among subject, object, and network such that what "counts" in writing and literature is the written text's conformity to interpretive norms, its ability to appeal to human senses, and to be decoded via ideological critique. In contrast with this established critical paradigm, Lin's *Heath* effectively simulates a contemporary Actor-Network reading environment, invoking ambience not as an ethereal abstraction but as an abundantly physical phenomenon. Tracing this contrast, Lin writes, "the 'idea of the book,' i.e. its formal materiality, often appears, at least when compared to the codex, as a dematerialized presence–what you call banal or readily overlooked material, but actually it's very specific forensically, and it often affects reading in a deliberate and pre-meditated way" (2009a).

The idea of an exteriorized ecosystem reflects a strand of current thinking weaving together ecology concepts with poetics, rhetoric, and media theory that, like Lin, is invested in the idea of ambience. In an early essay entitled "Why Ambient Poetics? Outline for a Depthless Ecology," Timothy Morton defines ambience as "a poetic enactment of a state of nondual awareness that collapses the subject-object division, upon which depends the aggressive territorialization that precipitates ecological destruction" (2002, p. 52).[20] Morton's definition of ambience illustrates how, far from being ethereal and apolitical, ambient writing is in fact an effective political act. From this perspective, we can see Lin's invocation of an exteriorized ecosystem of reading as an absolute rejection of the subject–object binary that permits the subordination of nonhumans to human desires. As Morton argues, the solution is to reject the anthropocentric linkage of intention and agency, writing, "a politics of the environment must be coterminous with a change in the view of those who exist in/as that environment. A poetry that articulated the person as environment

---

[20] Parallels between Morton's work in literary criticism and Latour's Actor-Network Theory abound: Morton is often associated with the Object Oriented Ontology movement, which is heavily influenced by Latour (Bryant et al. 2011, p. 2).

would not invert anthropocentrism into 'ecocentrism' but would thoroughly undo the very notion of a center" (2002, p. 54).[21] One of the ways in which an ambient poetics manifests this decentering is through the suppression of anthropocentric metaphor. As Morton writes, the conventional paradigm "treats the world as objective stuff to be manipulated by disembodied subjects, fostering subject-object dualisms of all kinds" (2002, p. 55). This reflects Lin's aspiration as stated in *BlipSoak01*: "Poems should be uninteresting and non-metaphorical enough to be listened to in passing or while 'thinking of something else'" (2003, p. 13). From this perspective, Lin's seemingly benign suggestion that poems should be non-metaphorical appears a radically political gesture that short-circuits "subject-object dualisms" and posits a kind of inside-out poetics, in which the book is comprised of whatever one is reading while "writing."

In another essay entitled "Ecology as Text, Text as Ecology," Morton characterizes this inversion as inhering in textuality as such. Morton writes, "Texts have environments. These environments are made of signs, yet the matter-sign distinction breaks down at a certain point, because one of these environments is *the* environment" (2010, p. 3, emphasis in original). With *Heath*, Lin is responding to precisely this point, performing in his poetics the environmentality of his own work: "It should now be obvious that for language to be truly relaxing it must usher from the things around us and not the things inside us" (1998, p. 38). Similarly, Morton writes, "No textuality can rigorously distinguish between inside and outside, because that is precisely what textuality both broaches and breeches" (2010, p. 3). What are the contents of *Heath*? The "book" is largely a record of Tan Lin's reading while working on the project and its revisions, of which there have been many. The most recent edition of *Heath* now includes an interview on the work and the abstract to Danny Snelson's article about *Heath* itself. All textuality is thus ambient textuality; what matters is the degree to which readers are made aware of the material contexts of the "work," the degree to which authors like Lin narrate their own dissolution into exteriorized ecosystems or networks.

What Lin and Morton make clear is that, as a theory of a mediational network, media ecology is resolutely anti-metaphorical. This argument is essentially an extrapolation from Morton's assertion about textuality: as with texts, media both *are* and *have* environments, and these

---

[21] Morton's suggestion that ambient poetics is decentering recalls the "pluralization" of agency in an Actor-Network methodology discussed above.

environments are composed of a heterogeneous assemblage of nonhumans and humans. Taking the words "media ecology" literally, we must shift how we think and talk about mediated relationality: we should cease to understand media ecology as "the study of media as environments" in the figurative sense that media operate *like* ecological systems (Postman 1970, p. 161).[22] Rather, we should approach media ecology as wholly non-metaphorical, acknowledging that media operate both *as* and *within* ecological systems. The literal ecosystem of reading that Lin invokes does not merely include texts that reference and are referenced by other texts but "a large company of authoring devices/genres/software programs/inks/printing technologies/fonts/ distribution systems/editorial practices/legal systems/legislative bodies and individuals" (2012a). We might also include paper mills, postal workers, Amazon.com warehouses, webmasters, and forests.

Such an ambient perspective radically disrupts the conventional definitions of both media and ecosystems, such that it is impossible to talk about them in isolation: media (as ubiquitous) are environmental, just as ecosystems are mediated. Far beyond bridging the nature–culture divide, a literalized media ecology disrupts the idea of individuation in general: "the idea of medium-specificity and discrete mediums … are being supplanted by the idea of a more general operating system or generic culture of software whose purpose is to continually redistribute a range of materials across a single platform" (Lin 2008, p. 96). In the place of a clearly demarcated poetry–prose dualism, for example, we now have Lin's *[AIRPORT NOVEL MUSICAL POEM PAINTING FILM PHOTO HALLUCINATION LANDSCAPE]*. A medium is simply a matter of perspective: that which is bracketed is interchangeable.

Similarly, media theorists Alexander Galloway and Eugene Thacker argue that "New media are not just emergent; more importantly, they are everywhere—or at least that is part of their affect" (2007, p. 10). In *The Exploit: A Theory of Networks*, Galloway and Thacker trace this complex process of de-individuation, redefining a network as, simply, "that which is ubiquitous" (2007, p. 10). Galloway and Thacker's work bears striking resemblance to Lin's, particularly in their emphasis on "the 'ambient' or the 'environmental' aspects of new media" (2007, p. 10). They write,

---

[22] This early essay, "The Reformed English Curriculum," features Neil Postman's first efforts at naming and defining media ecology. Notably, he advocates media ecology as a replacement for English curriculum.

> "Networks are elemental, in the sense that their dynamics operate at levels 'above' and 'below' that of the human subject. The elemental is this ambient aspect of networks, this environmental aspect—all the things that we as individuated human subjects or groups do not directly control or manipulate. (2007, p. 157)

Like Actor-Network Theory's insistence on the pluralization of agency, the ubiquity of networks in Galloway and Thacker's view subverts any attempt to locate intentionality, responsibility, or agency in any individual "node," such as a human subject. As Timothy Morton writes, "we are not ourselves" (2010, p. 7). When Tan Lin inscribes "Tan Lin," on the cover of *Heath*, he is not claiming absolute authority over the contents of the book but merely accounting for the fact that "Tan Lin" was one among many whose efforts produce, sustain, and continue to change *Heath*.

But Galloway and Thacker extend the Actor-Network methodology beyond this accounting, this tracing of agencies and counting participants in a network. They identify the true political efficacy in acknowledging the ambient aspects of networks, shifting the paradigm from critique to something else entirely. Resistance to the coercive nature of networks, for Galloway and Thacker, comes not in the form of a critic who stands outside the network and subjects it to a negative critique, revealing the hidden ideologies beneath the artifice, but in the form of a hacker who is embedded within the network, scanning for weaknesses—called "exploits" that can be turned against control societies from within (2007, p. 81). They write,

> A wholly new topology of resistance must be invented that is as asymmetrical in relationship to networks as the network was in relationship to power centers. Resistance *is* asymmetry. The new exploit will be an 'antiweb.' ... It will have to consider the radically *unhuman* elements of all networks. It will have to consider the nonhuman within the human, the level of 'bits and atoms' that are even today leveraged as value-laden biomedia for proprietary interests. (2007, p. 22)

This call to action emerges contemporaneously to Lin's *Heath*, evident in the similarities between the two projects. As Galloway and Thacker suggest, Lin's ambient poetics, far from abdicating the political project of the avant-garde, has merely turned to a different strategy: probing contemporary reading environments for points of weakness, for exploits, which can be turned against the network to subvert anthropocentrism by attuning reader-participants to the ambient agencies in the network.

Following Galloway and Thacker, it is my contention, ultimately, that "exploits"—hackable vulnerabilities in the system—depend on an emergent reading by collapsing the fallacious anthropocentric division between nonhuman passivity and human agency, subverting anthropocentrism in all its forms: sensory, textual, medialogical, critical, political (2007, p. 81). Where media's communicative potential fails, insight begins. This is a marked departure from Marshall McLuhan, whose work set the stage for decades of anthropocentric media theory as a set of effects on human subjects. Instead, the anti-reading emergent poetics demonstrates that media only "work us over completely" when we ignore the nonhuman aspects of the medium (McLuhan 1967, p. 26). Emergent poetics as resistance: against the hegemony of human senses, against media-prosthesis, against the exhaustion of negative critique, we can dislodge human subjectivity from its false dominion over literary criticism by tuning in to the ambient, environmental, nonhuman aspects of literary media.

References

Bryant, Levi, Nick Srnicek, and Graham Harman, eds. 2011. *The speculative turn: Continental materialism and realism*. Melbourne: Re.Press.

Cage, John. 2010. *Silence: Lectures and writings*. Middletown: Wesleyan University Press.

Emerson, Lori. 2014. *Reading writing interfaces: From the digital to the bookbound*. Minneapolis: University of Minnesota Press.

Gallagher, Kristen. 2010. The authorship of heath ledger in the new reading environment; on Tan Lin's *heath: Plagiarism/outsource*. *Criticism* 51 (4): 701–709. https://doi.org/10.1353/crt.2010.0007.

Gallagher, Kristen, and Chris Alexander. 2012. Kristen Gallagher and Chris Alexander with Christopher Schmidt. Interview by Christopher Schmidt. *The Conversant*. https://theconversant.org/staging/?p=82. Accessed 25 October 2016.

Galloway, Alexander, and Eugene Thacker. 2007. *The exploit: A theory of networks*. Minneapolis: University of Minnesota Press.

Goldman, Eric. 2006. Search engine bias and the demise of search engine utopianism. *Yale Journal of Law and Technology* 8 (1): 188–200. https://digitalcommons.law.scu.edu/facpubs/76. Accessed 25 October 2016.

Goldman, Judith. 2011. Re-thinking 'non-retinal literature': Citation, 'radical mimesis,' and phenomenologies of reading in conceptual writing. *Postmodern*

Culture 22 (1). https://pomoculture.org/2013/05/18/re-thinking-non-retinal-literature-citation-radical-mimesis-and-phenomenologies-of-reading-in-conceptual-writing-1. Accessed 4 June 2014.

Hansen, Mark. 2015. *Feed-forward: On the future of twenty-first-century media.* Chicago: University of Chicago Press.

Latour, Bruno. 2004. Why has critique run out of steam? From matters of fact to matters of concern. *Critical Inquiry* 30 (2): 225–248. https://jstor.org/stable/10.1086/ci.2004.30.issue-2.

———. 2005. *Reassembling the social: An introduction to actor-network theory.* Oxford: Oxford University Press.

———. 2012. *An inquiry into modes of existence: An anthropology of the moderns.* Cambridge: Harvard University Press.

Lin, Tan. 1998. Interview for an ambient stylistics. *Tripwire* 1 (1): 34–40.

———. 2003. *BlipSoak01*. Berkeley: Atelos.

———. 2007a. *Ambience is a novel with a logo.* Cambridge: Katalanche Press.

———. 2007b. *Bib.* Ubu Editions. http://p-dpa.net/home/wp-content/uploads/2019/11/Unpub_018_Lin_BIB.pdf. Accessed 11 October 2015.

———. 2008. Disco as operating system, part one. *Criticism* 50 (1): 83–100. https://jstor.org/stable/23130867.

———. 2009a. Tan Lin interviewed. Interview by Chris Alexander, Kristen Gallagher and Gordon Tapper. *Galatea Resurrects.* https://galatearesurrection12.blogspot.com/2009/05/tan-lin-interviewed.html. Accessed 23 June 2016.

———. 2009b. Plagiarism: A response to Thomas Fink. *Otoliths* 14. https://theotolith.blogspot.com/2009/06/tan-lin-plagiarism-response-to-thomas.html. Accessed 23 June 2016.

———. 2010. The BOMB intervw unedited 7000. Interview by Katherine Elaine Sanders. *Tanlin.* https://tanlin-blog.tumblr.com/post/522584846/the-bomb-intervw-unedited-7000. Accessed 23 June 2016.

———. 2012a. *Heath course pak.* Denver: Counterpath.

———. 2012b. Writing as a metadata container: An interview with Tan Lin. Interview by Chris Alexander, Kristen Gallagher, Danny Snelson, and Gordon Tapper. *Jacket2.* https://jacket2.org/interviews/writing-metadata-container. Accessed 11 October 2015.

McLuhan, Marshall. 1967. *The medium is the massage.* London: Bantam.

Morton, Timothy. 2002. Why ambient poetics? Outline for a depthless ecology. *Wordsworth Circle* 33 (1): 52–56. https://jstor.org/stable/i24039901.

———. 2007. *Ecology without nature: Rethinking environmental aesthetics.* Cambridge: Harvard University Press.

———. 2010. Ecology as text, text as ecology. *The Oxford Literary Review* 32 (1): 1–17. https://jstor.org/stable/44030819.

OED (*Oxford English Dictionary*). n.d.. https://www.oed.com. Accessed 27 June 2017.

Place, Vanessa. 2011. Kenning editions: Pamela Lu's *Ambient Parking Lot* and Tan Lin's *Insomnia and the Aunt*. Constant Critic. https://constantcritic.com/sueyeun_juliette_lee/kenning-editions-pamela-lu's-ambient-parking-lot-and-tan-lin's-insomnia-and-the-aunt. Accessed 23 June 2016.

Postman, Neil. 1970. The reformed English curriculum. In *High school 1980: The shape of the future in American secondary education*, ed. Alvin C. Eurich, 160–168. New York: Pitman.

Rickert, Thomas. 2013. *Ambient rhetoric: The attunements of rhetorical being*. Pittsburgh: University of Pittsburgh Press.

Sayes, Edwin. 2014. Actor–network theory and methodology: Just what does it mean to say that nonhumans have agency? *Social Studies of Science* 44 (1): 134–149. https://jstor.org/stable/43284223.

Scappettone, Jennifer. 2009. Versus seamlessness: Architectonics of pseudocomplicity in Tan Lin's ambient poetics. *Boundary 2* 36 (3): 63–76. https://doi.org/10.1215/01903659-2009-020.

Snelson, Danny. 2010. *Heath*, prelude to tracing the actor as network. Aphasic Letters. https://aphasic-letters.com/heath. Accessed 4 October 2015.

Stefans, Brian Kim. 2004. Streaming poetry. *Boston Review* 29 (5). https://bostonreview.net/articles/stefans-streaming-poetry. Accessed 4 June 2014.

Stephens, Paul. 2012. From the personal to the proprietary: Conceptual writing's critique of metadata. *Digital Humanities Quarterly* 6 (2). https://digitalhumanities.org/dhq/vol/6/2/000124/000124.html.

———. 2013. Vanguard total index: Conceptual writing, information asymmetry, and the risk society. *Contemporary Literature*, 54(4): 752–784. https://jstor.org/stable/43297934.

Thurston, Nick. 2013. *Of the subcontract*. Toronto: Coach House Books.

CHAPTER 5

Conclusion: Starting from Nothing

This project has positioned emergent poetics as a response to the hierarchies of human perception and an alternative institutional critique by emphasizing the aspects of texts—their material forms—that resist, rather than conform to, conventional modes of interpretation. In the first chapter, guided by the photogram-poetics of Susan Howe, emergent poetics allows us to uncouple technical media from human interpretation. In essence, Howe's poetry contravenes Marshall McLuhan's famous characterization of media as "the extensions of man," offering a broader view of the approach to written texts that shifts focus from those aspects immediately appealing to human perception toward the materiality of the texts that resists conventional interpretation. In the second chapter, Yedda Morrison's deep erasure of *Heart of Darkness* serves to reconceptualize networks of mediation as zones of emergence. By invoking the long-neglected concept of "biospherical egalitarianism" from the Deep Ecology movement, I argue that a reading informed by emergent poetics amounts to a kind of "bewilderment," or an experience of wilderness that belies the sovereignty of agential humanity over inanimate, passive nature. In the final chapter, I turned to the meta-theoretical concept of "ambience"—an environmental disruption of figure-ground, text-context binaries—in the poetry of Tan Lin to locate emergent poetics at the center of a theory of textuality for the twenty-first century, tracing the multiplicity of agencies at play in Lin's work and the ambient networks they simulate and into which they dissolve.

© The Author(s), under exclusive license to Springer Nature
Switzerland AG 2025
T. W. Matteson, *Emergent Poetics*, Modern and Contemporary Poetry
and Poetics, https://doi.org/10.1007/978-3-031-70737-7_5

As a final illustration of the critical aspirations of emergent poetics, I turn to Barbara Ehrenreich, whose recent memoir *Living With a Wild God: A Nonbeliever's Search for the Truth About Everything* in part details her youthful experiences with psychological fugues she now believes to be a kind of total dissociation. In a chapter entitled "The Trees Step Out of the Forest," Ehrenreich (2014) describes the first of such experiences, a moment when her body and mind forgot how to perceive:

> And then it happened. Something peeled off the visible world, taking with it all meaning, inference, association, labels, and words. I was looking at a tree, and if anyone had asked that's what I would have said I was doing, but the word 'tree' was gone, along with all the notions of tree-ness that had accumulated in the last dozen or so years since I had acquired language. Was it a place that was suddenly revealed to me? Or was it a substance—the indivisible, elemental material out of which the entire known and agreed-upon world arises as a fantastic elaboration? I don't know, because this substance, this residue, was stolidly, imperturbably mute. The interesting thing, some might say alarming, was that when you take away all human attributions—the words, the names of species, the wisps of remembered tree-related poetry, the fables of photosynthesis and capillary action—that when you take all this away, *there is still something left*. (p. 48, emphasis in original)

What is left, when anthropocentric perception melts away? When the names of things and their connotations no longer have any grip on the world? This, I suggest, is the sphere of inquiry germane to emergent poetics. Ehrenreich dissociative experiences (she does not consider it a disorder), as she describes them, seem to allow to her to be truly among things, to subvert description and categorization and to encounter the entirety of difference.

Not coincidentally, Ehrenreich describes the objects she encountered in her dissociative state as "mute," the same term Ponge uses in his title *Mute Objects of Expression*. Ehrenreich finds that, in Ponge's words, "The object is always more important ... it has no duty whatsoever toward me, it is I who am obliged to it" (2008, p. 4). The object's muteness is in fact coextensive with Ehrenreich's own muteness: this dissociation brings a sense of linguistic humility, as the perceiver is unable to name, describe, and thereby possess the object of her perception. But this is a different kind of muteness, a different kind of silence than Christopher Manes discusses in

"Nature and Silence": "Nature *is* silent in our culture (and in literate societies generally) in the sense that the status of being a speaking subject is jealously guarded as an exclusively human prerogative" (1992, p. 339). The silent treatment that Ehrenreich receives is not imposed by human culture, but is in fact a withholding, agential silence on behalf of the trees. That they are not *compelled* to speak their names, to conform to a linguistic category, is a kind of anthrodecentric inversion: it is Ehrenreich who is obliged to the trees, not the other way around.

How do we embrace such a deference to the nonhuman world? What is the poetics of anthrodecentrism? How can this perspective inform poiesis? Essentially, as Susan Howe says, we are "Starting from nothing with nothing when everything else has been said" (2010, p. 11). Ponge's poetics of co-nascence is one possibility, to attempt a co-birth between things and language by putting pressure on language's descriptive and nominative capabilities. Paula Claire's *Codesigns* (1976), a (similarly punning) work of poetry, offers another alternative. *Codesigns* is a collection of nine sight-sound poems intended to be composed in performance with an audience. As the above epigraph indicates, Claire's project returns us to a time anterior to language, to simulate the birth of language which, she suggests, is precipitated by a kind of synesthetic impulse to vocalize visual patterns in the natural world. This speculative score for collaborative performance was created using electron and optical microscopes, featuring magnified images of organic material, human skin, and other inorganic compounds. The poet and audience together compose vocalized soundscapes inspired by the contours of the microscopic images, essentially reinventing language.

These are, as the title suggests, "code-signs," to be sonically decoded in improvisational performance. Yet they are also "co-designs" in two senses of the term. On one hand, the poet invites the reader to be a participant, to co-design the work. On the other hand, the prefix "co-" recalls co-nascence: the microscopes, and the magnified objects themselves, are also co-authors: the "language" of the poem is anthrodecentric in that it defers to the object's contours, rather than imposing names and description. It is Claire and her human co-designers who are obliged to these nonhuman forms. Beyond the title, the individual poems in *Codesigns* also visually pun on language and poetics. For example, Claire includes an image of magnified skin cells from a human lip, a clever metonymic evocation of human speech.

Claire's *Codesigns* are a genealogical ancestor of an emergent poetics, exercising a reparative impulse, emphasizing positive affect and a tendency to, as Sedgwick puts it, "confer plenitude" on the generative objects of their poems. Emergent poetics are anthrodecentric, as the poet, readers, microscopes, and organic and inorganic materials are co-designers of the work. These poetics exhibit an affinity for nonhuman agencies in their tendency to assemble, attempting to account for the ways that even nonhuman agencies make a difference in the poetic process. Above all, emergent poetics offers a constructive alternative to negative critique, asking us instead to formulate a localized, immediate engagement with the world, an earnestly participatory assemblage, a true poiesis. To paraphrase Bruno Latour's "Compositionist Manifesto," do we not have enough ruins?

References

Claire, Paula. 1976. *Codesigns.* London: Writer's Forum.
Ehrenreich, Barbara. 2014. *Living with a wild god: A nonbeliever's search for the truth about everything.* New York: Twelve.
Howe, Susan. 2010. *That This.* New York: New Directions.
Manes, Christopher. 1992. Nature and silence. *Environmental Ethics* 14 (4): 339–350. https://doi.org/10.5840/enviroethics19921445.
Ponge, Francis. 2008. *Mute objects of expression.* Trans. Lee Fahnestock. Brooklyn: Archipelago Books.

Index[1]

A
Actor-Network Theory, 9, 11–13, 84, 95–100, 99n18, 103, 103n20, 104n21, 106
Ambience, 103, 111
Anthrodecentrism, 11–14, 40, 52, 78, 113, 114

B
Bennett, Jane, 2, 3, 7–9
Biocentrism, 14, 51, 54, 55, 58, 62, 64, 68–70, 72–77
Blanchot, Maurice, 25n8
Bogost, Ian, 7–9, 72
Brakhage, Stan, 69–74, 77
Bruns, Gerald, 1–3, 10, 27, 28, 30, 31, 37

C
Cage, John, 65n8, 88, 88n7

Carson, Rachel, 62, 74, 75
Claire, Paula, 113, 114
Codesigns, see Claire, Paula
Conrad, Joseph, 8, 14, 51, 53–56, 58, 60, 63, 69

D
Darkness, see Morrison, Yedda
Dworkin, Craig, 18n1, 42

E
Erasure poetry, 14, 52, 59–62, 64

F
Frolic Architecture, see Howe, Susan

G
Goldsmith, Kenneth, 2

---

[1] Note: Page numbers followed by 'n' refer to notes.

H

Hansen, Mark, 12, 13, 39n18, 85
Heath: Plagiarism/Outsource, see Lin, Tan
Howe, Susan, 10, 14, 46, 52, 62n7, 66n9, 111, 113

J

Johnson, Ronald, 59, 60, 63–70

L

Lacan, Jacques, 4n1
Latour, Bruno, 1, 3, 13, 95, 95n13, 96, 98, 100, 100n19, 103n20, 114
Lin, Tan, 10, 14, 83–107, 111

M

McCaffery, Steve, 7n3, 65, 66, 68
McLuhan, Marshall, 12, 19, 20, 73, 107, 111
Media ecology, 2, 11, 83, 89, 104, 105, 105n22
Morrison, Yedda, 8, 10, 14, 51–79, 111
Morton, Timothy, 2, 3, 14, 84, 103, 103n20, 104, 104n21, 106
Mothlight, see Brakhage, Stan

N

Naess, Arne, 77, 77n13, 78
Nonhuman, 8, 11, 13, 14, 35n14, 51, 62, 63, 72–76, 89, 100–102, 106, 107, 113, 114

O

Oelschlaeger, Max, 51n1, 52, 62, 75–78

P

Parikka, Jussi, 12, 13
Photograms, see Welling, James
Ponge, Francis, 3–10, 4n1, 4n2, 7n3, 10n4, 112, 113
Post-critique, 1, 8, 9, 11–13, 17, 20, 89, 96–98, 106, 107, 111, 114

R

Radi os, see Johnson, Ronald
Reparative reading, see Sedgwick, Eve Kosofsky

S

Schweitzer, Albert, 75, 75n12
Sedgwick, Eve Kosofsky, 11, 13, 17, 97, 98n17, 114
Sharif, Solmaz, 61, 62
Silent Spring, see Carson, Rachel
Snelson, Danny, 84, 87n5, 89, 90, 91n10, 95, 96, 99–101, 104
Stefans, Brian Kim, 90, 91, 95
Stein, Gertrude, 56
Stevens, Wallace, 35n15, 46

T

Telepathy, 14, 18, 24, 35–39, 39n17, 41, 44
That This, see Howe, Susan
Thoreau, Henry David, 31, 31n10, 32
Thurston, Nick, 87

W

Welling, James, 5, 14, 17, 21–23, 23n6, 26, 28–30, 32, 33, 38, 43

Z

Žižek, Savoj, 9, 10

Printed in the United States
by Baker & Taylor Publisher Services